D1059436

# Oh, the Deep, Deep Love of Jesus

# Oh, the Deep, Deep Love of Jesus

## Expository Messages from John 17

Michael A. Milton, Ph. D.

Wipf and Stock Publishers
Eugene, Oregon

Wipf and Stock Publishers
199 West 8th Avenue, Suite 3
Eugene OR 97401



Oh, the Deep, Deep Love of Jesus: Expository Messages from John 17

By Michael A. Milton, Ph. D.



1st edition.

ISBN 13: 978-1-59752-218-2

# Dedication

For Pastor Bob and Marylu Baxter

And always for Mae

# CONTENTS

# ACKNOWLEDGMENTS

Maximizing the Word of God preached is an essential core value of my ministry. To do this requires a team of selfless servants of the Lord. I want to acknowledge their efforts, friendship and collaboration. Thanks toWipf and Stock Publishers for agreeing to produce this volume and other sermon series for readership; to Ron Brown, Russ Hightower, Helen Holbrook, Geoff McDowell, Sandy Pierce, Rankin Wilbourne, and Steve Wallace for their expert pastoral and supervisory work and their assistance in shepherding the flock; to Mrs. Martha Miller, Mrs. Joye Howard; and to our session and deacons for their support of the vision. Thanks to my friend and hero in the ministry, John Guest, for writing the introduction. Thanks to Ben Haden for his commitment to pray for his unworthy successor. Thanks to the inspiring congregation of First Presbyterian Church. Each and every Lord's Day, the sight of you all causes me to thank God for the true honor of being your pastor. And thanks to Mae and John Michael who have shared in each message reproduced here in many ways.

For a magical time in my life, during the early days of 2005, I got to spend time, with my family and our congregation at First Presbyterian Church of Chattanooga, Tennessee, meditating upon the deep, deep love of Jesus. It is my prayer that the Lord will use this series of Bible messages to draw you into the glorious presence of Christ in worship and experience His love personally.

# INTRODUCTION

It is an amazing thing to enter into the "Holy of Holies" with the Lord Jesus and hear Him bare his heart and speak face-to-face with His Heavenly Father. It is an amazing thing to hear the Lord Jesus sum up His work on earth in prayer, when you realize that work was "foreordained from the foundation of the world" (1 Peter 1:20). It is an amazing thing to hear the Lord Jesus praying to the Father when you realize that "He reflects the glory of God and bears the very stamp of his nature, upholding the universe by his word of power" (Hebrews 1:3).

Dr. Michael Milton wonderfully takes us into these profound mysteries. Three things strike me as I read his work, *Oh, The Deep, Deep Love of Jesus.*

The first is his reverence for the text of John 17 and his brilliant exegesis of the same. For one who has read it many, many times and preached from it over a lifetime of ministry, the writing of Dr. Milton is refreshing and scintillatingly relevant. His writing style is crisp and clear and draws the contemporary reader into the world and content of this ancient prayer.

Secondly, his use and selection of quotes from other writers, both ancient and modern, brings a wealth of study and research to the text. For any minister or teacher of God's word, this becomes a tremendous resource, as well as a personal inspiration.

Thirdly, you sense in Dr. Milton, who himself is a preaching pastor, a world of experience in the understanding he brings to the human heart and condition which every preacher must address. His illustrative material both draws out the meaning of what the Lord Jesus was praying, and incisively directs and applies it to the everyday experiences of the reader.

All told, Dr. Milton's work, *Oh, The Deep, Deep Love of Jesus*, makes a profound contribution to the body of literature that over the years has taught about the High Priestly Prayer of Jesus. That he would take the words from the great hymn, "Oh, The Deep, Deep Love of Jesus" and use them to describe the Lord Jesus praying at the institution of the Last Supper, is, all by itself, a powerful invitation to enter into that prayer.

> O the deep, deep love of Jesus, vast, unmeasured, boundless, free!
> Rolling as a mighty ocean in its fullness over me!
> Underneath me, all around me, is the current of Thy love
> Leading onward, leading homeward, to Thy glorious rest above!

**The Rev. Dr. John Guest**

"This is truly, beyond measure, a warm and hearty prayer. He opens the depths of His heart, both in reference to us and to His Father, and He pours them all out. It sounds so honest, so simple; it is so deep, so rich, so wide, no one can fathom it."

**Martin Luther**

"There is no voice which has ever been heard, either in heaven or in earth, more exalted, more holy, more fruitful, more sublime, than the prayer offered up by the Son to God Himself."

**Phillip Melanchthon**

# 1

# JESUS' PRAYER OF COMPASSION

## John 17:1-13

We can know the words and forget the music. We need to recover the music of romance with the gospel by recovering a relationship with Jesus.

One way to recover that relationship is to come into contact with the love of Jesus through one of the most extraordinary prayers ever uttered: the High Priestly Prayer of Jesus in John 17. As we begin this study, my prayer is that we will so immerse ourselves in the truths of this prayer that we will not only know the words of Christianity but also the music of Christianity.

After instituting the Lord's Supper and commanding His disciples to love one another and facing the cross of sacrifice, Jesus prayed.

> When Jesus had spoken these words, he lifted up his eyes to heaven, and said, "Father, the hour has come; glorify your Son that the Son may glorify you, since you have given him authority over all flesh, to give eternal life to all whom you have given him. And this is eternal life, that they know you the only true God, and Jesus Christ whom you have sent. I glorified you on earth, having accomplished the work that you gave me to do. And now, Father, glorify me in your own presence with the glory that I had with you before the world existed. "I have manifested your name to the people whom you gave me out of the world. Yours they were, and you gave them to me, and they have kept your word. Now they know that everything that you have given me is from you. For I have given them the words that you gave me, and they have received them and have come to know in truth that I came from you; and they have believed that you sent me. I am praying for them. I am not praying for the world but for those whom you have given me, for they are yours. All

mine are yours, and yours are mine, and I am glorified in them. And I am no longer in the world, but they are in the world, and I am coming to you. Holy Father, keep them in your name, which you have given me, that they may be one, even as we are one. While I was with them, I kept them in your name, which you have given me. I have guarded them, and not one of them has been lost except the son of destruction, that the Scripture might be fulfilled. But now I am coming to you, and these things I speak in the world, that they may have my joy fulfilled in themselves" (John 17:1-13).

## PODS WITHOUT PEAS?

I spent many a humid summer evening on the back porch of our little croft in the backwoods of Louisiana. While on that back porch, I shelled a lot of peas. Every now and then I would get a big pod, pretty as anything, but with no peas in it. Of course, I would throw those aside. However, if you get too many of those, you know you've got a problem with your crop.

As the husk without the kernel inside, so can we have form without internal power. The result is a loss of authenticity. Pastor and people alike can confuse form and truth. We can be a bunch of pods with no peas.

From time to time we should ask ourselves, Is this a real relationship with a real Jesus, or is this just religion? The answer has to do with having a personal knowledge of the love of Jesus Christ in your life.

An old Puritan named Traill once said,

> The secret moth and poison in many people's religion is, that it is not Christianity at all. God out of Christ is a consuming fire; God not worshipped in Christ is an idol; all hopes of acceptance out[side] of Christ are vain dreams...[1]

Francis Shaeffer put it like this:

> Biblical orthodoxy without compassion is surely the ugliest thing in the world.[2]

[1] J. C. Ryle, *Expository Thoughts on the Gospels: John* (Carlisle, PA: Banner of Truth Trust, 1987) John, vol 3, 198.

[2] http://www.goodtheology.com/inventory.php?target=quote"eformat=all#Compassion.

A man can master all of the branches of systematic theology, can memorize many key verses, can know the flow of the history of God's people from Adam to Billy Graham, but if he is without a loving relationship with Jesus Christ, then the secret moth and poison of lovelessness has rendered his religion powerless.

I want to draw your attention to John 17. One ancient scholar said of the prayer of Jesus contained in this chapter,

> There is no voice which has ever been heard, either in heaven or earth more exalted, more holy, more fruitful, more sublime, than this prayer.[3]

This prayer has three major movements. In John 17:1-5, there is a movement of prayer in which Jesus prays for Himself. In John 17:6-19, He prays for His disciples, and then in John 17:20-26, Jesus prays for all believers.

But we must be careful here, as in all Scripture, about divisions. The great Anglican Bishop of Liverpool, in his wonder over this prayer, said,

> He that reads the words spoken by one Person of the blessed Trinity to another Person, by the Son to the Father, must surely be prepared to find much that he cannot fully understand, much that he has no line to fathom.[4]

So we come to this passage in wonder. I remember standing at the top of the Empire State Building with my wife and son a few years ago. The wind was blowing, and we held on to each other as we peered out over the ledge to one of the greatest cities on earth. What grandeur as we looked at the other buildings and all of the people below! We looked away from Manhattan to the great harbor and all of the ships. What a sight! But the sight in this part of God's Word is even greater! The experience of seeing the Grand Canyon or the Pacific coastline or the beauty of our own mountains cannot compete with the vision of the Son of God bowed in prayer, about to die for His people, speaking in intimacy with His heavenly Father about a covenant made between Father and Son before the stars were ever flung into space! What a sight! We can

[3] Ryle, 194.
[4] Ibid., 188.

divide this into portions, but the whole of it is indivisible and in some way unimaginable. Again, Ryle says,

> There are sentences, words, and expression, in the twenty-six verses of this chapter, which no one probably has ever unfolded completely.[5]

I pray you can feel, as I did in dealing in with this magnificent prayer, like Isaiah coming into the throne room of God and crying,

> ..."Woe is me! For I am lost; for I am a man of unclean lips, and I dwell in the midst of a people of unclean lips; for my eyes have seen the King, the LORD of hosts!" (Isaiah 6:5).

I want you to see that John 17 is purifying for your life. As we look at the character of the prayer and the compassion of Jesus in the prayer, I hope it leads us to a conviction in our own lives.

## The Character of Jesus' Prayer

The character of this prayer is seen in its substance.

### The character is unique

There is nothing else like it. It is the longest recorded prayer of Jesus. The church is right in referring to this as the High Priestly Prayer because Jesus, having instituted the Lord's Supper and having shown that He is the Lamb to be slain for the people of God, the fulfillment of the Passover, now shows that He is the Priest to offer the sacrifice for righteousness and the atonement for sin. He is both Lamb and Priest. Life and eternal life is given only through Him. Now He goes to His father with your name, my name, names not yet named on earth, and the names of all of those ancients who trusted in God's plan of salvation.

### The character is victorious

This is a victory prayer. Calvin Miller, in *The Christ We Knew*, writes,

> Jesus celebrated the victory before the decisive battle. He gloried in all that He would shortly finish—all that God had called Him to do. The dying still lay ahead of Him, but the purpose for his living on earth in time was all finished.[6]

[5] Ibid.

[6] Calvin Miller, *The Christ We Knew: Eyewitness Accounts from Matthew, Mark, Luke, and John ; with 31 Days of Devotions* (Nashville, TN: Broadman & Holman Publishers, 2000).

### The character is deep

As we come to this scene, creation, fall, and redemption converge at the sight of the Son of God lifting His eyes to God the Father and praying a prayer that will lead to His atoning death and sacrifice for sinners. In this prayer there is something afoot that human minds cannot fully understand. We look at this the way we look at a newborn baby or a man and woman in love or the way I looked at the Tennessee gorge off of Signal Mountain this morning. I see it. I experience it. But it is, in a way, too great for me to comprehend. Luther said,

> ...this prayer sounds plan and simple, it is in reality deep, rich, and wide, that which none can fathom.[7]

Yet the prayer is not so deep that you cannot be moved, that you cannot discover the love of God for your life in it. It is filled with a depth of love that woos us and draws us into the scene.

### The character is intimate

The character is not only deep, it is also intimate. It is intimate with God the Father. It is intimate as John, and perhaps all of the disciples, were able to listen to this prayer. It is intimate as we are welcomed into this holy communion between Father and Son and listen as our names are mentioned, for He prays for those who will believe through the testimony of the disciples.

I used to get so excited when I went to court my wife that I had to take breathing exercises in order to see her! Then after seeing her, I couldn't go to sleep! It is called being lovesick, I believe.

John 17 is a courtship between Jesus and your soul. He and His Father bid you to come and be one in this prayer, to be lovesick with the Lover of Your Soul. May you never get over it.

## The Compassion of Jesus' Prayer

Every great love must first be rooted in a covenant relationship. Love without covenant is fleeting, Hollywood-like, without strength to endure.

[7] Ryle, 194.

## Jesus' compassion is rooted in covenant

> When Jesus had spoken these words, he lifted up his eyes to heaven, and said, "Father, the hour has come; glorify your Son that the Son may glorify you..." (John 17:1-2).
>
> "And now, Father, glorify me in your own presence with the glory that I had with you before the world existed" (John 17:5)

The love and compassion of the Lord Jesus Christ is rooted in the triune love of God—Father, Son, and Holy Spirit eternally dwelling together in the fellowship of love and compassion.

In John 3:16 Jesus says it—"For God so loved the world, that he gave his only Son." Here in John 17:1 Jesus prays it. This is the gospel. This is love for a world of sinners who will be redeemed by Christ Jesus the Son. All of the love shown on Calvary begins in the unity of Father, Son, and Holy Spirit.

In John 10, the great Good Shepherd chapter, we see this same love rooted in covenant.

> "My sheep hear my voice, and I know them, and they follow me. I give them eternal life, and they will never perish, and no one will snatch them out of my hand" (John 10:27-28).

But now listen to this:

> "My Father, who has given them to me, is greater than all, and no one is able to snatch them out of the Father's hand" (John 10:29).

There it is. The people of Christ are preserved because of the relationship of a sacred agreement between God the Father and God the Son now made known.

The spirit of God has allowed you to eavesdrop on a conversation between God the Son and God the Father speaking of the bond of love and the eternal covenant that existed before the foundation of the world when the Son existed with the Father in all of His glory before He took upon the flesh. There a covenant was made that the Father would give as a gift to the Son those of you who have trusted in Jesus Christ. We begin to see that all of the love and compassion of the universe is held together, not by my love, not by my faith, not by what I do, but by the love of God in Christ. All the universe is being held together by the plan of God. Unfathomable, yes. But it is given to us that we may know the assurance of eternal life—all that You have given Me. You are a gift of God the Father to God the Son before the earth was formed. God sent his Son Jesus Christ to provide the righteousness that the Father required in His plan and to die an atoning death. That is what this prayer is about. Your salvation is secure if you have trusted in the Lord Jesus Christ because it is not about you; it is about the gift of God the Father to God the Son. The compassion of Jesus is rooted in the love for the Father.

## Jesus' compassion is revealed in ministry

Jesus prays for Himself; He prays about what He has done.

> "I have manifested your name to the people whom you gave me out of the world....I have given them the words that you gave me.... I am praying for them....I am no longer in the world..." (John 17:6-11).

Here is the compassionate ministry of Jesus Christ. He came to show us the love of Almighty God. He is love personified. He came to give the truth about God's plan of salvation. He gives eternal life to all whom the Father has given Him.

The great Puritan John Owen wrote,

> We are never nearer Christ than when we find ourselves lost in a holy amazement at his unspeakable love.[8]

We are drawn to Christ in this prayer, and we come to see that in His ministry of coming to live for us and die for us and pray for us, His very person is the essence of compassion for His people.

## Jesus' compassion is reaching out to His people

Jesus begins by praying to the Father. Then our Savior begins to pray for those the Father has given Him. He prays for His disciples.

> "I have manifested your name to the people whom you gave me out of the world" (John 17:6a).

Beginning in John 17:20, He prays for you, also.

[8] http://www.gracegems.org/8/Holy%20amazement.htm

> "I do not ask for these only, but also for those who will believe in me through their word, that they may all be one, just as you, Father, are in me, and I in you, that they also may be in us, so that the world may believe that you have sent me. The glory that you have given me I have given to them, that they may be one even as we are one, I in them and you in me, that they may become perfectly one, so that the world may know that you sent me and loved them even as you loved me" (John 17:20-23).

In Luke we see the compassion of Jesus for the widow of Nain who lost her child.

> Soon afterward he went to a town called Nain, and his disciples and a great crowd went with him. As he drew near to the gate of the town, behold, a man who had died was being carried out, the only son of his mother, and she was a widow, and a considerable crowd from the town was with her. And when the Lord saw her, he had compassion on her and said to her, "Do not weep." Then he came up and touched the bier, and the bearers stood still. And he said, "Young man, I say to you, arise." And the dead man sat up and began to speak, and Jesus gave him to his mother. Fear seized them all, and they glorified God, saying, "A great prophet has arisen among us!" and "God has visited his people!" And this report about him spread through the whole of Judea and all the surrounding country (Luke 7:11-17).

In this story, we see the love of Jesus as He leaves the crowds to minister to the one. This is the personal compassion of Jesus Christ for our needs. We see the love of Jesus as His heart went out to her. Jesus is for us, not against us. Today, the widows can know that Jesus' heart goes out to them. The little child who feels alone, who feels that no one understands her struggle with her lessons at school, can know that Jesus loves her and His heart goes out to her. The one who is sick needs to know that the heart of Jesus goes out to him. The businessman who is worried about his business is the object of Jesus' affection. The couple without a child, the teenager with searching questions, the empty nest couple struggling to find meaning in their lives again are all objects of His compassion. He is for the prostitute who sees her condition. He is for the adulterer who is broken in his sin. He is for the young man who wants to propose and for the young woman who waits. He is for the family gathered at the graveside, and He is for the doctor seeking to bring healing at the surgical table.

But in Jesus, we not only have compassion—and the tender heart of the Almighty God of the universe is no small thing—but healing flows from His hands. Jesus raised her son from the dead! In Jesus we not only have a God who wept over Jerusalem, but one who died for sinners and said, "Father, forgive them for they know not what they do!"[9] We not only have a Savior who is compassionate at the graveside, but a Savior who will one day open the grave and call them to heaven, body and soul!

Jesus speaks to your condition; and he not only has compassion for you, but he works miracles. He moves in your heart, and He creates out of nothing something glorious and wonderful in your life.

## The Conviction of Jesus' Prayer

What does this passage do to you? What does the sight of the Son of God praying to His Father for His disciples and then naming your name do for you? It should convict you. There should be a passion arising within you that responds to the passion you see in Jesus and the compassion that He has for you.

This kind of compassion which was demonstrated in Jesus' prayer leading to His death for sinners, leading to God's descending into the grave, leading to His resurrection and ascension and coronation as Lord of all in heaven, leading to His Spirit being poured out on His people for worldwide ministry coming down to this very movement, must have a profound effect upon our hearts and our wills.

This kind of compassion must surely produce a harvest filled with peas in the pods. This kind of love, this meeting with this Jesus, will produce authentic faith or will show us to be unbelievers.

Thomas Brooks put it so clearly:

> Miss [Christ] and you miss all.[10]

But know Christ, know His love and compassion in your life, and you have all.

[9] Luke 23:34
[10] http://www.puritansermons.com/previous.htm

### This compassion should convict the unbeliever

In John 17, Jesus Christ mentions the word "world" numerous times. Each time He uses it, save for one, He is speaking about the system of unbelievers who oppose Him or ignore Him in this age. As an unbeliever, if you remain in your unbelief, if you remain afar from Him, He does not pray for you.

> "I in them and you in me, that they may become perfectly one, so that the world may know that you sent me and loved them even as you loved me" (John 17:23).

If I were an unbeliever listening to Jesus pray about the world saying, "I am not praying for the world," and I came upon this passage, I would be clinging to the passage "that the world may know." He is not praying for me because I do not believe in Him, but He is praying that the world may know through those who do believe. I would be convicted to say, "I want to be of that number. I do not know this kind of love and power in my life apart from this Man of Nazareth. I want this prayer to be for me." Peter says, "Make your calling and election sure."[11]

Jesus Christ is praying for those who are His. Confirm that you are His by repenting of your sin, by believing in your heart that Jesus is the Savior you need to forgive your sin, by confessing that He died for your sin and that God raised Him from the dead. I charge you before God to confess Him as your Lord and Savior.

### This compassion should convict the believer

As you look at the love of God in Christ about to go to the cross, it should convict you if there is a lack of love. God has allowed you to listen to the words of this prayer. He prays for those who will believe through the testimony of those first disciples. That is you and me. Shall Jesus' compassionate prayer not move us to love Him, to give our all to Him, to resist the devil and the flesh, and to rest in His covenant made with His heavenly Father? Shall this not cause us to say, "How may I respond in love to this Lover?"

[11] 2 Peter 1:10

## CONCLUSION

There have been many affected by this prayer, but my mind goes to that brave Scotsman, John Knox. I went to a seminary that bears his name. His vision of "Give me Scotland or I shall die" is to be the creed of every graduate of that school. "Give me America or I shall die," says the pastor in America. "Give me the Sudan or I shall die," says the missionary there.

But for those who do not know the life of John Knox, that may sound like bravado. We learn about what matters most to a man at his deathbed. When John Knox lay dying, after a life of preaching Christ, of bringing the gospel to bear in his native land, of suffering as a slave to the French, of being persecuted by his own rulers in Scotland and in England, he asked his wife to read from that place where he first cast his anchor. She read from John 17.

At the grave of John Knox a mourner remarked, "Here lies one who neither flattered nor feared any flesh." What was the power behind that kind of Christian? What gave John Knox the power that caused Mary Queen of Scots, who opposed the reformed faith, to say, "I fear the prayers of John Knox more than all the assembled armies of Europe"?[12] What was the vision that led this man to give his life away for generations he would never see so that true faith would be established in his homeland, that led Knox to cry, "Give me Scotland or I shall die"? It was the love of Jesus for John Knox. It was not bravado. It was compassion.

Paul, too, knew this love. It was the secret of his power, and so at the end of his life Paul would write,

> For I am already being poured out as a drink offering, and the time of my departure has come. I have fought the good fight, I have finished the race, I have kept the faith (2 Timothy 4:6-7).

And what will cause us to follow Him all the way? To seek to serve Him in our lives in our generation? Will it be our strength of convictions or our character or even our faith? No. It will be the love of Jesus for our

[12] Charles H. Sylvester, ed., *Progress of Nations* (Hanson-Bellows Company, 1912) vol. III, pp.454-457, http://www.forerunner.com/forerunner/X0525_Bios-_John_Knox.html.

sin-sick, hell-deserving soul. It will be the unfathomable love of Jesus praying our names to His Father as He went to die for us.

Will you now say, "Give me Jesus or I shall die?" The eternal destiny of your soul and the destiny of many around you await your response.

# Questions for Reflection

1. What did you understand to be the "romance of the gospel"? How does Jesus' prayer of compassion renew that romance in your own life with God?

2. Does the chronology of this prayer, in relationship to the Lord's Supper and the great commandment to love one another, help us in understanding the ministry of Jesus? How?

3. Name the ways in which this prayer of Jesus is different than the prayer in Gethsemane.

4. Which passages in the prayer speak to the covenant relationship between Father and Son? How do those passages affect your life this very moment?

5. In what ways does this prayer strengthens believers?

6. In what ways does this prayer reach out to the lost?

## Prayer

Lord, whose love became flesh in Jesus, I am amazed at your great love shown to me in this wonderful prayer. Thank you for revealing your heart for your people in this prayer. Help me to live with assurance as a result of this prayer. Help me to live out of the grace you have shown to me and share your grace with others. In your Name, O Christ.

*Amen.*

"The passages of Scripture which prove that the instrument of our sanctification is the Word of God are very many. The Spirit of God brings to our minds the precepts and doctrines of truth, and applies them with power. These are heard in the ear, and being received in the heart, they work in us to will and to do of God's good pleasure. The truth is the sanctifier, and if we do not hear or read the truth, we shall not grow in sanctification. We only progress in sound living as we progress in sound understanding. 'Thy word is a lamp unto my feet and a light unto my path.' Do not say of any error, 'It is a mere matter of opinion.' No man indulges an error of judgment, without sooner or later tolerating an error in practice. Hold fast the truth, for by so holding the truth shall you be sanctified by the Spirit of God."

Charles Haddon Spurgeon

# 2

# If the Truth Be Known

## John 17:14-19

We really do want to know the truth.

Jesus tells the truth. He not only tells the truth, but in John 17, He prays that you would know the truth.

> "I have given them your word, and the world has hated them because they are not of the world, just as I am not of the world. I do not ask that you take them out of the world, but that you keep them from the evil one. They are not of the world, just as I am not of the world. Sanctify them in the truth; your word is truth. As you sent me into the world, so I have sent them into the world. And for their sake I consecrate myself, that they also may be sanctified in truth" (John 17:14-19).

## There Must Be More

Let's suppose you are in a courtroom and you have been called to the witness stand. The clerk gives you a Bible and asks you to raise your right hand and repeat, Do you solemnly swear to tell the truth, the whole truth, and nothing but the truth. As the judge and the jury look at you, you reply, "Well, that all depends upon what you mean by 'truth'."

That won't work! However, in reality, that could be a possible answer in our generation.

We are said to be living in a postmodern age. I believe this is not only true but is affecting how we as believers must retool in order to relate the gospel of Jesus Christ to a world in transition. The very nature of postmodernism defies a clear description, but Stanley Grenz, in *Primer on Postmodernism*,[1] helps us understand what a postmodern worldview is. Postmodernism, at its essence, is a destruction of modernism. Dr. Spock, the pointed-eared character on "Star Trek," was the quintessential modern. He had an answer, a rational answer, for everything. That is modern man. But the horrors of the twentieth century have ravaged the human soul so that rational answers no longer make sense. There must be more.

A Christian worldview actually has some things in common with postmodernism because we, too, reject a purely modern answer. In a word, we also believe that there is more to the answer of human pain. But where modernism rejected the supernatural answers, postmodernism embraces all answers as valid—except any that are exclusive. And this is the rub.

Christianity says there is one great story—the old, old story of creation, fall, and redemption—and that Jesus Christ himself says that there is truth.

When He stood before Pilate, Jesus claimed truth for Himself; and Pilot asked, "What is truth?" Philosophers have asked, What is truth? What we know as postmodernism has been around through the centuries. But how does the gospel go forward, and how do we live in that arena?

Jesus says that there is truth. In fact, in John 17 Jesus prays for truth. John 17 is not one truth competing with other truths. It is the overarching mind of God that is revealed through Jesus and brings hope and healing to the world.

What does this Scripture teach us that Jesus believed about His truth? If the truth be known, you might say, Jesus prayed for truth for us because He cares for us. Let's look at the power of this truth.

[1] Stanley J. Grenz, *A Primer on Postmodernism* (Grand Rapids, Mich.: William B. Eerdmans Pub. Co., 1996).

## The Truth Can be Known

In John 17:14 Jesus said, "'I have given them your word.'" In John 17:17 He says, "'Your word is truth.'" So according to Jesus, it not only can be known, but it must be known or He would not have prayed for it.

### The truth about the word "truth"

In the New Testament there are two great words for truth. One is the word *amen*. In John, Jesus uses this word when he says, I am about to tell you something that is true. He says, A*men*, *amen* (the King James translates it, Verily, verily), I say unto thee. That *amen* is a declaration that what I am about to say corresponds with reality. It may be a reality you don't understand, but a reality that is, nevertheless, there.

The other word is *aletheia*. *Aletheia* is the word Jesus uses in John 17. This word is used over a hundred times in the New Testament, and it speaks of disclosure of that which has been concealed. This is the absolute pristine revelation—in this case, of God in the person of Jesus Christ.

In John we learn two things about *aletheia*.

- Truth is personal

Jesus Himself is truth. Jesus has prayed that His disciples would know the truth and He says, "Your word is truth."

> The Word became flesh and made his dwelling among us. We have seen his glory, the glory of the One and Only, who came from the Father, full of grace and truth [aletheia] (John 1:14, NIV).

In John, Jesus said that *alethia* will set you free.[2] He also said that He is the way, the *aletheia*, and the life.[3] Jesus is the very personification of truth. He is the full disclosure of God. In Colossians Paul says that Jesus Christ is the fullness of the Godhead bodily.[4] In one verse in Revelation, we see how the person of Jesus Christ is both the *amen* and *aletheia*; both are used in one verse:

---

[2] John 8:32
[3] John 14:6
[4] Colossians 2:9

> "And to the angel of the church in Laodicea write: 'The words of the **Amen**, the faithful and **true** witness, the beginning of God's creation" (Revelation 3:14).

Robert Browning, in *The Ring and the Book*, wrote,

> I thirst for truth,
> But shall not drink it till I reach the source.[5]

In the Bible Jesus, the person, is the source of truth. I believe that our greatest apologetic, our defense of the Christian faith and what we believe, begins in the person of Jesus Christ. To know truth is to know Jesus Christ.

- Truth is propositional

Truth is not only personal with Jesus, it is propositional.

Some like to hear about Jesus the person but do not want to hear about the propositions, the teachings, the mind of God, which is between Genesis and Revelation. But Jesus says that this, too, is true.

When Jesus was raised from the dead, He taught disciples on the road to Emmaus by opening and interpreting the Scriptures in order to show them that the Christ was taught in the Old Testament and in order to reveal Himself. Jesus is truth personally, but we also know truth propositionally.

In John 17:17 Jesus says, "'Your word is truth.'"

D.A. Carson is exactly right when he asserts that the gospel "is virtually incoherent unless it is securely set into a biblical worldview."[6]

Jesus is truth, but He is the Word, and the Word became flesh, and the Word is revealed in truth that can be taught from the Scriptures.

When Timothy faced the monumental task of revitalizing a congregation facing enormous challenges, Paul advised him,

> But as for you, continue in what you have learned and have firmly believed, knowing from whom you learned it and how from childhood you

[5] Robert Browning, "The Ring and the Book," *The Complete Poetical Works of Robert Browning*, Ohio University Press 1988, vol. 8, vi. 2038, p. 165 as cited by William Sykes, *The Eternal Vision: The Ultimate Collection of Spiritual Quotations* (Peabody, MA: Hendrickson Publishers, Inc. 2002) 441.

[6] D.A. Carson, *The Gagging of God: Christianity Confronts Pluralsim* (Grand Rapids, MI: Zondervan, 1996), 502.

> have been acquainted with the sacred writings, which are able to make you wise for salvation through faith in Christ Jesus. All Scripture is breathed out by God and profitable for teaching, for reproof, for correction, and for training in righteousness, that the man of God may be competent, equipped for every good work (2 Timothy 3:14-17).

You can know the truth by reading the truth. The truth is recorded for us in the Word of God. In times past prophets spoke, but now we have the final Word through the Lord Jesus Christ. What we have as the Bible is the truth.

John Piper wrote in *Desiring God* that the Bible is your kindling for joy. You know what kindling is—you gather your wood and that is the start of a fire. The Bible is the kindling of our joy

I remember the Bible teaching of my Aunt Eva as I sat in her lap. I could hear her heart beat as she prayed and as she read the Scriptures. Her heartbeat mingled with the Scriptures so that love and truth and relationship were woven together in my heart. And though I would wander far from the truth, it was that truth in love, that heartbeat of the gospel from her lap of love that, like a beacon of light, like a radar signal, began to lead me home. This is what Jesus is praying about.

My beloved, let us cherish the Word of God in our families, for to cherish the truth of the Bible is to cherish Jesus. Truth cannot be divided. He is the Word, and He is to be found in every part of the Word of God. He is on every page. So let us teach the children early about the truth of Jesus. Let us also speak the truth in love to each other and to the world. Let us not become entangled in a world that will not speak truth or is hesitant to speak truth. But let the truth come out of prayer, out of relationship, and let our own heartbeat be in it.

Clearly, this truth that Jesus teaches about is in conflict with modernism because modernism lives in the rational. To have God send His only begotten Son to save sinners from their sins is not rational. This truth is also clearly in conflict with postmodernism because in saying that He is truth, Jesus is claiming, "Let God be true and every man a liar"[7] He is saying that He is

[7] Romans 3:4

truth, His Word is truth, and this *aletheia* is unique, non-negotiable, propositional, and clear.

So can the truth be known? In the face of all other competing philosophies and worldviews and religions, Jesus says, Yes. I am truth, and My Word is truth.

Now we see why He prays for truth for His disciples.

## For If the Truth Be Known...

If the truth can be known, and it can be, it can have powerful consequences.

### If the truth be known, then the truth will SAVE.

"I have given them your word..." (John 17:14).

How are disciples made into disciples? It is through the gift of the Word of God.

The true Word, which is a gift, transforms the human soul. It has a power unlike any other power. It is the very breathed out Word of God. We are regenerated by the Word and become the sons and daughters of God.

This truth is given to all who by faith hear the Word, understand the truth of the Word—that we are sinners in need of a Savior and that Jesus Christ alone is the unique way to be forgiven by God and adopted to be children of God. There is no other. And you not only see this truth, but surrender to it and call on Jesus as your living Lord and Savior.

### If the truth be known, then the truth will SEPARATE.

If, as we see in Jesus' prayer, there are two classes of people—those who are saved and those who are not—then the truth separates. It separates truth from error. It separates in order to distinguish the truth from the error. It doesn't just say that you are that way and must stay that way. It divides and then says, Come and know the truth and be healed.

In John 17:14 we read

> "...and the world has hated them because they are not of the world, just as I am not of the world" (John 17:14).

Again in John 17:16 it says

> "They are not of the world, just as I am not of the world" (John 17:16).

Looking back at John 17:9,

> "I am praying for them. I am not praying for the world but for those whom you have given me, for they are yours" (John 17:9).

It is, therefore, indisputable. Jesus' prayer shows how the truth of the revelation of God about man's plight and about God's power separates the believer from the unbeliever.

Some years ago Albert Schweitzer, in *Christianity and the Religions of the World,* noted

> "...Christianity, in the contest with philosophy and with other religions, should not ask for exceptional treatment, but should be in the thick of the battle of ideas, relying solely on the power of its own inherent truth."[8]

Amen. Never before in the history of the world do we have more of an opportunity to witness to the truth of Jesus Christ. Why? Because the lines are drawn so clearly. Our culture, as filthy as it is getting, nevertheless, allows for seeing sin for sin and truth for truth. As God overcame Baal on Mount Carmel with Elijah and the pagan prophets, Christ will overcome every contest for the hearts and minds of men. Jesus will be victorious, and we must never be afraid in this world or ashamed of the gospel "...for it is the power of God for salvation to everyone who believes...".[9]

**If the truth be known, then the truth will SEAL.**

> "I do not ask that you take them out of the world, but that you keep them from the evil one" (John 17:15).

[8] Albert Schweizer, *Christianity and the Religions of the World,* translated by Joanna Powers, Geroge Allen and Unwin, 1924, p. 18 as cited by William Sykes, *The Eternal Vision: The Ultimate Collection of Spiritual Quotations* (Peabody, MA: Henrickson Publishers, 2002) 442.

[9] Romans 1:16

This is what Paul meant when he wrote to the Philippians, seeking to encourage them.

> And I am sure of this, that he who began a good work in you will bring it to completion at the day of Jesus Christ (Philippians 1:6).

It is reminiscent of the words of Jesus in John 10:29.

> "My Father, who has given them to me, is greater than all, and no one is able to snatch them out of the Father's hand" (John 10:29).

The truth of the gospel is that the power of God not only saves you but seals you. John said to believers in 1 John,

> But you have an anointing from the Holy One, and all of you know the truth (1 John 2:20).

Jesus is our Mediator and High Priest, and when Jesus prays that we will be kept by the truth, you can be sure the truth of the gospel will keep you.

The truth of the gospel is that while we were still sinners, Christ died for us. The truth of the gospel is that our broken spirits and vulnerability, coming out of our awareness of our sin condition, opens the door of God's strength in Jesus Christ. And likewise, this truth is what keeps us. Knowing Jesus and His grace saves us and seals us.

**If the truth be known, then the trust will SANCTIFY.**

Our Lord prayed,

> "Sanctify them by the truth; your word is truth" (John 17:17, NIV).

And then He says again,

> "For them I sanctify myself, that they too may be truly sanctified" (John 17:19, NIV)

The Greek word for sanctify is *hagiazo*. It is to set apart, to make holy, a dedication of one's self to God.

To be sanctified is to have the power of Almighty God accessible to you through word, sacrament, and prayer so that you may know the mind of God and you may be increasingly conformed to the image of Jesus.

Simply, sanctification is wanting what God wants, hating what God hates, and loving what God loves in this world.

Thus, Jesus is saying that He is consecrating Himself to the cross, and He is praying that you will know the truth that will sanctify you, preserve you, keep you, grow you, and prepare you.

### If the truth be known, then the truth will SEND.

"As you sent me into the world, I have sent them into the world" (John 17:18, NIV).

Jesus is praying for His disciples that they may go into the world the way He came into the world and that they may bring the truth into the world and that the truth would be like a fragrance diffused throughout the world. This is the plan of God. The truth is not something that we hold tightly and don't share. In fact, those who have been possessed by this truth, are possessed in order to be sent. It is a bubbling over, it is a response to that love in a sending out into the world.

His truth is not content to be with a small group of people who have it all together. His truth is intended to go to people who know they are in need, and then, out of gratitude for what God has done for them, they have disclosed this truth to others.

One of the greatest lies to come into the church in the twentieth century is that of universalism. That doctrine says that all will be saved eventually, so there is no reason to send. That one lie infected the mainline denominations in an unprecedented way. From 1953 to 1980, the overseas missionary force of mainline protestant denominations of North America decreased from 9,844 to 2,813. Thank God, those Christian groups who still believe that men are lost without Christ and can only be saved by the preaching of the Word, increased during the same period by 200%.

If the truth be made known to my heart, I must share it. If the truth is known to the church, the church can't stand away from the world; the church must go into the world. Let us not miss this: if the truth is known, it must be sent.

What a great responsibility comes to us, as a new generation, taking the gospel into the twenty-first century. I have been thinking about how we ought to have a passion to get the truth out. I give you three Rs to remember.

**Recruit** workers for our harvest fields. Here Jesus prays for us to be sent. In another place, Jesus said that we should pray for workers for God's harvest. This is what I mean by recruiting. We should be sounding the alarm that our Savior calls us to go tell others. Let every one of us consecrate ourselves to being used of the Lord to reach others for Jesus Christ in this world in our time. There is no greater calling, and it is upon each and every one of us. We much challenge each other in personal evangelism, in short-term missions, in supporting the work of missions in the church. We must be passionate about people being sent.

**Reseed** the gospel, scattering the seed where it has been scattered before. It came up; but now lies, errors, heresies have infected the ground of Western civilization and other ideas have become prominent. We need to reseed the gospel by evangelizing Europe and America where once the gospel grew green grass. Our hearts must not only break, we must go and tell the truth to the West. Let's work and pray for church planting in the barren areas of our nation and also in the barren areas of the West. Old Christendom, like Europe, awaits a revival. We must pray, work, and enter movements and networks where the faithful exposition of the gospel is taking place. We must be sent to reseed.

**Reach** the frontiers. Preach where nobody has preached before.[10] Using every agency and every means available to us, we must reach the ends of the earth with the gospel. This is why Jesus was sent by His Father, and this is our vocation as well—to preach the gospel of Jesus Christ to those who have never heard. There are immigrant groups in our nation which must be reached. Out of the 12,000 or so ethno-linguistic groups on earth, there are still some who have not heard, where there is no church planting movement. We must locate them and get the gospel to them. If the truth be known, we must go.

[10] John Piper, *Desiring God: Meditations of a Christian Hedonist* (Sisters, Or.: Multnomah Books, 1996) 191.

## CONCLUSION

Jesus is praying for truth. The truth, despite all other claims, can be known and when known, has powerful consequences. The truth saves, it separates, it seals, it sanctifies, and it sends. But it all begins by knowing the source of truth—Jesus Christ.

The One who prays for you is the source of truth. If He, the Truth, be known, you will not possess the truth. The Truth will possess you and never let you go.

And that is what this prayer is really all about.

# Questions for Reflection

1. Think about how Jesus prays concerning the truth. How is Jesus' understanding of truth different from the way truth is talked about today?

2. What does this prayer have to do with the doctrine of the inerrancy and infallibility of the Bible?

3. How do we know what Jesus knows? How much can we know that Jesus knows?

4. How does Jesus' truth change a person? How does this prayer change you?

## Prayer

Father of truth, release me from the limitations of not knowing your truth. In the midst of a generation that personalizes truth and, thus, distorts it, help me to breath in your truth and to share it with others. Lord Jesus, you are truth. In Jesus' name.

*Amen.*

"Few souls understand what God would accomplish in them if they were to abandon themselves unreservedly to Him and if they were to allow His grace to mold them accordingly."

**Ignatius**

"The question in salvation is not whether Jesus is Lord, but whether we are submissive to His lordship."

**John MacArthur**

# 3

# Four Myths about Submission in the Christian Life

## John 17:1-8,13

Paul Miller, the author of *Love Walked Among Us*, begins teaching seminars by writing these words on a flip chart:

> I do nothing on my own. I can only do what I see my dad doing.

He asks for analysis. In the age of Oprah and Dr. Phil, the armchair psychologists' answers come:

> He sounds weak. Almost helpless.
> Does he have a mind of his own?
> If he's an adult, he needs a little separation from his dad.
> Has this person been to counseling?
> Not healthy.
> Very childlike.
> He's codependent.

Miller writes, "After I've let the hook go deep, I tell them that Jesus said those words."

> ..."I tell you the truth, the Son can do nothing by himself; he can do only what he sees his Father doing, because whatever the Father does the Son also does....By myself I can do nothing..." (John 5:19, 30, NIV).

Jesus is the model of submission. Consider the submission of Jesus in His High Priestly Prayer and what it says to us today. May the hook of

God's grace go deep and reel us in to see just how dependent we are...and how wonderful that is.

> When Jesus had spoken these words, he lifted up his eyes to heaven, and said, "Father, the hour has come; glorify your Son that the Son may glorify you, since you have given him authority over all flesh, to give eternal life to all whom you have given him. And this is eternal life, that they know you the only true God, and Jesus Christ whom you have sent. i glorified you on earth, having accomplished the work that you gave me to do. And now, Father, glorify me in your own presence with the glory that I had with you before the world existed. "I have manifested your name to the people whom you gave me out of the world. Yours they were, and you gave them to me, and they have kept your word. Now they know that everything that you have given me is from you. For I have given them the words that you gave me, and they have received them and have come to know in truth that I came from you; and they have believed that you sent me" (John 17:1-8).
>
> "But now I am coming to you, and these things I speak in the world, that they may have my joy fulfilled in themselves" (John 17:13).

## WE WILL HAVE NO KING TO RULE OVER US

"Where am I missing it?" As a British pastor now ministering in the United States, that was the question John Guest was asking himself. He felt that he was not connecting with his parishioners in Pennsylvania. He was a fine preacher, an excellent scholar, and a very friendly and engaging personality. He was also very devoted to Jesus Christ and to preaching His Word. One weekend as he was antiquing with his wife, he found his answer, the missing link of understanding in his ministry. The answer was printed on a Revolutionary-era sign that he spotted in an antique shop. The sign, which would have hung in a Colonial general store, read, We will have no king to rule over us! John Guest came to understand that he had come from England where having a king, calling someone Your Lordship, was a part of the culture. But the idea of lordship and total monarchy was something completely outside of the American psyche.

That independent spirit created a great nation. But it can get in the way when it comes to submitting your life to another in relationships like marriage, friendship, work, but especially and primarily in a relationship with God. Nothing could be more central to the Christian life than the creature submitting himself to His Creator.

We are considering submission in John 17 because it is at the very heart of this prayer. In this prayer Jesus is perfectly submitted to His Father. He calls God His Father, and this speaks of submission. Jesus says that He is doing what the Father wants Him to do, and this speaks of submission. In seeing this submission, there are messages for our lives as His people. Submission is not popular for a people bent on self-identity, self-realization, and self-reliance, but God calls us to a life of submission, and we can learn something about it from this passage.

I want to address four myths about submission in the Christian life.

## Myth 1—Submission to God Is a Loss of Freedom.

Many people believe that if they submit their lives to the Lord Jesus Christ, they will lose their freedom, they cannot do anything that they want to do in life. A tragic flaw in this reasoning is that a person who is not under the lordship of Jesus in not free. The Bible says that you are in bondage to sin, to the lusts of your own flesh, to the whims of an evil spiritual opponent who wishes you destroyed, and to a world that is alienated from the one who brings true freedom. Or as that great theologian Bob Dylan put it,

> You're gonna have to serve somebody,
> Well, it may be the devil or it may the Lord
> but you're gonna have to serve somebody.[1]

This myth then precipitates another lie: You can be a disciple of Jesus without a radical submission to Jesus in every area of your life. This desire to have it both ways took on a very seductive heresy a few years ago when we heard about Jesus being our Savior but not our Lord. This is a lie. If He is not Lord, He is not Savior.

I want to show you that Jesus, while being God, was in total submission to God the Father.

[1] http://bobdylan.com/songs/serve.html

He claimed to be God, and there can be no mistake about it. In John 10:30 He claimed that He and the Father were one. The religious leaders plotted against him because He claimed to be God. He said that if you have seen Him, you have seen the Father. Yet this one who is God, who claims divinity,[2] who says in John 17 that He was with the Father before the world ever began,[3] also says that He does only what the Father wants Him to do.[4] He is submissive to God His Father. His being is perfectly equal, but His role is submissive.

This prayer of Jesus in John 17 shows total submission. Even the opening of His prayer shows this.

> After Jesus said this, he looked toward heaven and prayed, "Father, the time has come. Glorify your Son, that your Son may glorify you" (John 17:1, NIV).

The phrase "the time has come" is meant to say that His appointed time to die for the sins of His people has come. Jesus is living a life that His Father ordained for Him. He is headed for the cross to die for sinners. Yet, there has never been anyone more free because our Lord is controlled by a love that He said existed before the world began. He is free from every other passion and interest because of His one holy passion. And one holy passion makes you free.

Shall you think that you, a mortal, a creature created by this God, can maintain independence by being alienated from this God? Can you, believer, actually think for one moment that you, who are said to be a gift of love from Father to Son, can actually be independent from God? Going your own way? But many imagine such a thing.

The classic tale of resisting God for his own supposed independence is that of the great church father Augustine. In his *Confessions* Augustine recounts how he did not want to yield his life to God, thinking that do so would be to give up his own rights. But the prayers of his mother,

---

[2] "I and the Father are one" (John 10:30).

[3] "And now, Father, glorify me in your own presence with the glory that I had with you before the world existed" (John 17:5).

[4] So Jesus said to them, "Truly, truly, I say to you, the Son can do nothing of his own accord, but only what he sees the Father doing. For whatever the Father does, that the Son does likewise" (John 5:19).

Monica, and the words of a child drove him to the Scriptures where he saw the insanity of unbelief. Augustine wrote these words:

> You called, you cried, you shattered my deafness.
> You sparkled, you blazed, you drove away my blindness.
> You shed your fragrance, and I drew in my breath and I pant
> for you.[5]

That is the language of a lover and a heart set free.

I resisted God in my own life. Perhaps like someone reading this, I thought that to live apart from God meant freedom. But it was insanity. I was deaf to the sound of His sweet words of life. I was blind to the sight of His hand moving in my life and in the world. I had no sense of the presence of God. But to give your life away to the Lord is to be acquitted of the judgment against your sins and to be set at liberty. And more. it is not only to know Him but to experience His power in your life. It is, in a word, to live.

Now let me address this matter to the believer. This myth, shed at the point of receiving Christ as Lord and Savior, re-appears, like a virus, in the Christian life. The myth reappears whenever Christ calls you to follow Him into a new calling, to a new role in His kingdom. It is then that we say, I don't want that kind of restriction in my life. I, too, remember being called to follow God into the very narrow calling of the ministry. I told God that I could serve Him just as well in other ways. I even felt that to follow God into this calling would be to restrict my life. Then, a friend told me about the life of Martin Luther. Luther was gifted to be a great lawyer or a great musician, but Luther said that because he was called to preach, he was in chains. But in his chains he found his freedom.

Yes, my beloved Christian friend, to follow Jesus to teach that class, to go to the mission field, to surrender to God to be a pastor, or to follow Him to forgive that one who hurt you, will put you in chains. But in those velvet chains of Jesus Christ, you will find your freedom. Submission to the Lord is not a loss of freedom but a life of liberty like you have never known before.

---

[5] http://www.avatarmeherbaba.org/erics/staugust.html

## Myth 2—Submission Is a Loss of Identity

Again, we must point to the fact that in submitting to His Father, Jesus does not lose His identity as God, but his role relationship with the Father is clarified.

> "I have brought you glory on earth by completing the work you gave me to do" (John 17:4, NIV).

Yet there are some who think that if they follow Jesus, they will lose their identity as freethinking, do-as-they-please people. Or they think they will check their minds at the door of the church and be mindless robots. How far from the truth this is. Yet how many secretly hold on to this lie of hell.

What is the answer? The answer is love. Jesus submitted to His Father in a covenant of redemption made in eternity past to leave His royal robes of divinity to live as man and to die for man that man may live. He submitted Himself to earthly authorities, even though all of them—kings and parents and governments—will one day have to bow their knee to declare that Jesus is Lord to the glory of God the Father. Jesus submitted Himself to the elements of the world—the dreary dampness of the rainstorm and the scorching heat of the sun—even though He created the elements out of His own word. He submitted Himself to the cross even though He made the trees from which that cross was formed. He submitted Himself to evil men and then cried, "Father forgive them..."

Why? Because He was intent on saving the gift given to Him by His Father before the foundation of the world. You are a gift of love from God the Father to God the Son. Jesus' identity is the Son and your identity is a child of God, if you submit to Jesus.

I tell the men who come to me to be married that in taking this woman to be your wife, you are giving up your identity as your own man. You are now entering a life where you live for this woman. You will become, in the eyes of God, one flesh with her. You are to give your life away to her. I tell the woman that in taking his name, in becoming his wife, you are submitting to Him as a believer does to Christ. I remind them that Sarah called her husband Lord. Sometimes that one throws them a bit. No, it never does when they are in love and committed to each other. Submission is no problem where there is love.

Years ago I heard the motivational speaker Zig Zigler. I like him. He is from Mississippi and used to be a salesman. He gives sage advice, especially to salesmen. When I was a manager for Ashland Chemical, I took my salesmen to hear him. He said a lot of good things that really helped us, but the thing I remember most was his introduction of himself. He said, "Hi, I am Mrs. Zigler's happy husband!" I have since used that line many times. "I am just Mae Milton's happy husband." "I am John Michael Milton's happy daddy." Why say that? You know why. Love. Love delights in assuming the identity of the one loved, in marriage, in friendship, even in work.

My friend, giving your life to the Lord Jesus Christ will not be a loss of identity. Submission is a sweet surrender that brings sonship.

> Hi, I am the forgiven sinner, the slave set free, the happy child of the One I love.

## Myth 3—Submission Is a Loss of Purpose

> "For you granted him authority over all people that he might give eternal life to all those you have given him" (John 17:2, NIV).

Jesus has a very narrow purpose. He is the Mediator of the Covenant. He is the High Priest, holy and unblemished, to go before the Father to present us righteous. He is the Lamb of God to be slain for the sins of His people. "You shall call His name Jesus for He shall save His people from their sins."[6] This is a very limiting role. Paul's letter to the Philippians speaks about how He submitted to His Father's will:

> And being found in human form, he humbled himself by becoming obedient to the point of death, even death on a cross. Therefore God has highly exalted him and bestowed on him the name that is above every name, so that at the name of Jesus every knee should bow, in heaven and on earth and under the earth, and every tongue confess that Jesus Christ is Lord, to the glory of God the Father (Philippians 2:8-11).

[6] Matthew 1:21

Submission to God the Father caused Jesus to realize His purpose.

Jesus tells us that when we are crucified to self, we live. He tells us that whoever saves his life will lose it and whoever loses his life for Jesus' sake finds it. Thus, A.W. Tozer wrote,

> People who are crucified with Christ have three distinct marks:
> 1. they are facing only one direction,
> 2. they can never turn back, and
> 3. they no longer have plans of their own.[7]

And Bonhoeffer rightly said,

> When Christ calls a man, He bids Him come and die.[8]

But to die to sin, to the old self, is not to lose your purpose for life. It is to find it.

If you ever get tired of my six sermons on John 17, please remember that Martyn Lloyd-Jones has four volumes on John 17! This man, Lloyd-Jones, is one of the most fascinating figures in twentieth century church history. This Welshman from humble beginnings in South Wales was trained as a physician at St. Bartholomew's in London, a noted medical school and training ground for world-class doctors. He became a surgeon and was, in fact, an official surgeon to the British monarchy. His wife, also, was a physician. But God called Him to the ministry. He left St. Bartholomew's and the staff of the Queen to preach the gospel to coal miners in South Wales. The *London Times* ran a feature story on this. The whole angle was, How could a prominent young London physician possibly leave all the money and trappings and respect and honor of his position to give his years to poor coal miners in Wales. His answer? "I gave up nothing. I gained all. It is an honor to preach the gospel of Jesus Christ."

I used to think that if I followed the Lord, I would lose my purpose. The thing is, I didn't know what my purpose was. It kept changing. But since Jesus took control of my life, He gave me a purpose. As a husband, a father, a friend, a worker, a human being with emotions and desires

[7] http://psalm121.ca/quotes/dcqtozer.html.
[8] Dietrich Bonhoeffer, *The Cost of Discipleship* (New York, NY: Collier Books, 1963) 99.

and interests, I now have a purpose: to offer my life to Jesus as an act of love. When I do, I receive great delight and joy. If I died today, I would be a most complete man. My completeness no longer depends on what great things I have done. I am free from that. My completeness is in Him. I am like a wife in love with her husband. I am like a child who looks up to a father and finds identity in Him.

I have lost nothing in following Him. I have realized peace and fulfillment. And you will, too. For submission to the Lord is not a loss of purpose. Submission to His will is the great destiny of the happiest people on earth.

## Myth 4—Submission Is Loss of Joy

This myth says that if I become a Christian or if, as a Christian, I follow the Lord to where I believe He is calling me, I will no longer be happy. This is one of the greatest lies.

Jesus prayed that his disciples might know joy.

> "But now I am coming to you, and these things I speak in the world, that they may have my joy fulfilled in themselves" (John 17:13).

Jesus also says,

> "I made known to them your name, and I will continue to make it known, that the love with which you have loved me may be in them, and I in them" (John 17:26).

To welcome Jesus into your life, to follow Him, to give all away for Him, is to know the joy and love of the Triune God in your own life. You were, in fact, created that you may glorify Him and enjoy Him.

John Piper says of the love of the Triune God,

> In creation God "went public" with the joy that reverberates between Father and Son."[9]

In the fall of man, our ears became deaf and our hearts became cold to that reverberating joy. But in new birth, in redemption, we can hear again. We can feel again. We are like smokers who quit and can suddenly

[9] John Piper, *Desiring God* (Sisters, OR: Multnomah, 1996) 44.

taste again. And the longer we linger before Him in prayer and in His Word, the tastier His joy becomes.

The question is this: Are you really satisfied not having the ultimate joy that your heart craves? Are you content with living below the line of joy?

I think of the words of CS Lewis at this point:

> We are half-hearted creatures, fooling about with drink and sex and ambition when infinite joy is offered us, like an ignorant child who wants to go on making mud pies in a slum because he cannot imagine what is meant by the offer of a holiday at the sea. We are far too easily pleased.[10]

For too long, as a young man, I was too easily pleased. But I was most miserable. I sought and sought to find joy. Yet, to think that I would find it by giving away my life seemed, at minimum, a contradiction to me. It may to you. My friend, I have never known such joy as following Jesus Christ.

Would you be satisfied today clinging to half-hearted dreams? Would you walk away content with the little trinkets of this world when eternal life is offered? Would you be pleased with anything less than knowing and following this Jesus who prays for His own?

Submission to the Lord Jesus is not a loss of joy, but a mending of the woundedness of our souls that brings endless delight to our lives.

## CONCLUSION

Recently the attention of the nation has been riveted on the case of Terri Schiavo. You know the story. In 1990 Terri was found unconscious in her home having suffered brain damage after her heart stopped. Some have said that she is in a persistent vegetative state. Others believe that she is in a minimally conscious state.

Her husband, who has lived with another woman for ten years, is seeking a court order to remove the feeding tubes and essentially starve her to death. Here is what amazes me: Bob and Mary Schindler will not

[10] C.S. Lewis, *The Weight of Glory and Other Addresses* (Grand Rapids:Eerdmans, 1965), pp. 1-2 as cited by John Piper, *Desiring God* (Sisters, OR: Multnomah, 1996) 17.

give up. Where there is a question of life in their daughter, they choose to err on the side of life. I would stand with them to the end on that premise. It is the Christian response to stand for life where there is a question of life. But here is what I am getting at. Their lives have been totally surrendered to their daughter's life for all of these years. They live for the slightest twinkle in her eye. They kiss her and hold her and turn her and love her. Their love for her has put their own needs and their own dreams into the background. They live to see her live. When her brother, Bobby, was asked about everything that he has given up and gone through to keep her alive, said,

> "I don't regret a second of what we've been through." He said that it will all be worth it "when we save my sister."[11]

Jesus submitted his life to His Father to die so that we who were given to Him by His Father can live, even though we die.

To surrender your life to Jesus Christ will not be a hard choice if you know His love and receive it. You may face trials and even persecution for surrendering your life to Jesus Christ. But on the day when the prayers of Jesus for you are finally answered and you are safe in the arms of Christ, you will look at it all and say, "I don't regret a second, it was all worth it…to see Him now.

[11]Associated Press Writer Mitch Stacy, *Schiavo Legal Fight Could Be Nearing End* [Internet] (Saturday February 26, 2005 7:16 PM 2005 [cited February 26, 2005 2005]); available from http://www.guardian.co.uk/worldlatest/story/0,1280,-4828022,00.html.

# Questions for Reflection

1. How is the concept of submission addressed in John 17?

2. The first myth is that submission to Christ is a loss of freedom. Have you ever felt that as God was calling you to a life of faithful discipleship to Christ? What have you lost? What have you gained in this submissive relationship to Him?

3. The second myth deals with a supposed loss of identity. Having read the chapter, articulate how Jesus is God yet submissive as the Son. How does His identity to His father relate to your identity as His child?

"The lesson before us [in John 17] is full of comfort and instruction. It is evident that Jesus sees far more in His believing people than they see in themselves, or than others see in them."

Bishop J.C. Ryle

# 4

# Five Facts of True Christian Faith

## John 17:20-23

Author Anne Lamott says that the greatest prayers she has ever heard were, "Help me! Help me! Help me!" and "Thank you. Thank you. Thank you." She says that within the context of those words is a distinctively powerful, biblical, Christian theology that says, I need God. The only place I can get my needs met, eternally and temporally, is through the Lord Himself. He meets those needs, and it liberates me to live a life of gratitude.

We can learn a lot through prayer. In four potent verses of John 17, we see the facts of faith according to Jesus.

> "I do not ask for these only, but also for those who will believe in me through their word, that they may all be one, just as you, Father, are in me, and I in you, that they also may be in us, so that the world may believe that you have sent me. The glory that you have given me I have given to them, that they may be one even as we are one, I in them and you in me, that they may become perfectly one, so that the world may know that you sent me and loved them even as you loved me" (John 17:20-23).

### Keep the Faith

These days we hear a lot about faith—faith groups, faith communities, faith-based programs. People say, "just have faith" and "keep up the faith." But what is faith? Take a look around and you will find that the use of the word faith often does not mean faith in Jesus Christ. For instance—and this is a classic—Sharon Salzberg is cofounder of the Insight Meditation Society and author of *Faith: Trusting Your Own Deepest Experience*. In the introduction to her book, Salzberg writes,

> I want to invite a new use of the word faith, one that is not associated with a dogmatic religious interpretation or divisiveness. I want to encourage delight in the word, to help reclaim faith as fresh, vibrant, intelligent, and liberating. This is a faith that emphasizes a foundation of love and respect for ourselves. It is a faith that uncovers our connection to others, rather than designating anyone as separate and apart.
>
> Faith does not require a belief system, and is not necessarily connected to a deity or God, though it doesn't deny one. This faith is not a commodity we either have or don't have—it is an inner quality that unfolds as we learn to trust our deepest experience.[1]

According to Salzberg —and the popular usage of the word faith in much of culture today—faith that is tied to a belief system or God or theological dogma is just not "fresh, vibrant, intelligent and liberating." This is the seductive siren song of this present age, and every one of us must see it for what it is. And for what it is not.

One way to do this is to study the prayer of Jesus. In His prayer, Jesus prays essential truths about faith.

> "I do not ask for these only, but also for those who will believe in me through their word" (John 17:20).

The word for believe is also the word for faith. He prays for those who would believe in Him through their (the disciples) word. So He is praying for you. He is praying that you will believe. In fact, the meaning in the Greek is that you will keep on believing. He is not only praying for your salvation, he is also praying for your sanctification. He is praying for a faith that will keep you through eternity.

It is definable. In fact, in this prayer of the Lord Jesus Christ, there are five distinctive facts about faith. In a world where faith has no descrip-

[1] "The Meaning of Faith" [Internet] (American Public Media, 2004 [cited March 3 2005]); available from http://speakingoffaith.publicradio.org/programs/2003/04/11_faith/.

tion, where faith is kind of a cuddly feeling, where faith is a faith in no god or any god, Jesus prays for a specific faith for your life. Jude talks about "the faith that was once for all delivered to the saints."[2] This faith is the sum of the teachings, the system of belief, taught in the Word of God. This is the faith that Jesus is praying for.

## True Faith Begins with the Prayer of Jesus

The first fact of faith in the Christian life is that God has taken the initiative to come to you. The first fact of faith is that Jesus is seated in the heavens praying for those the Father gave to Him from the foundation of the world. He is praying for you, and true faith begins with prayer.

Jesus prayed for his disciples, and here he prays for those who will believe through their word. That's you and that's me.

A man in our congregation tells me that he is a believer because every day of his life, his mother prayed for him. His life took all kinds of turns, but the prayers of his mother brought him home. The truth of the gospel is that the Lord moved on his mother to pray, and behind this mother's prayers, was the prayer of Jesus moving through a mother to lift up her little boy.

Today someone is praying for a son or a daughter or a parent or a friend. Behind your prayer is the prayer of Jesus Himself moving your prayer up to the throne of God. Jesus prays for you.

Jesus told Peter how Satan wanted to sift him, but Jesus said, "I have prayed for you."[3] So when you are going through trials, do not forget that you are covered by the prayers of Jesus.

Hebrews says that Jesus ever lives to intercede for us. Jesus is praying today that some hearts will be prepared to receive this faith by receiving Jesus. You may not receive Him today. You may resist. But He is preparing you. Others have already experienced the preparing ministry of Jesus. Maybe you were reared by a godly parent, maybe you read a book that pointed you to Christ, but now here you are and Jesus' prayers for

[2] Jude 3
[3] Luke 22:32

you will come to fruition today. Wherever you are, whatever you are doing, He is praying for you.

In Job 1:6 and following, we see Satan going before the throne of God, and He is asking for Job. In John 17, Jesus goes before His Father, and He asks for you. Satan may want to come against you, difficulty and trial may come against you, but Jesus has prayed for you.

True faith begins, not with me taking the initiative, but with a prayer of Jesus Christ.

## True Faith Is a Response to Testimony

"I do not ask for these only, but also for those who will believe in me through their word" (John 17:20).

The way we believe is through the testimony of Jesus' disciples.

When I was commissioned an officer in the Army, I received what is called a "direct commission." My name, along with others, went before the president, and I assume his pen machine signed my commission. But it is called a direct commission.

The apostles received a direct commission from Jesus Christ. They were commissioned to speak in the name of Jesus, heal in the power of Jesus, and establish the foundation of a worldwide church in the authority of Jesus. These men saw Jesus face-to-face. And our faith is established upon their faith.

> So then you are no longer strangers and aliens, but you are fellow citizens with the saints and members of the household of God, built on the foundation of the apostles and prophets, Christ Jesus himself being the cornerstone (Ephesians 2:19-20).

That foundation is the Word of God. The Spirit of God moved upon the prophets and upon the apostles, and through their testimony, the Word of God has gone through the centuries to us today. Any believer who has been transformed by God, loves God's Word.

One of my favorite poems is Robert Burn's "A Cotter's Saturday Night." A cotter was one who lived in a cottage, in other words, a typical Scotsman and his family. Burns speaks of the "priest-like father" taking the old Bible in his hands and reading it to his "bairns" and teaching them the Word of God. And Burns writes,

> From scenes like these old Scotia's grandeur springs,
> That makes her lov'd at home, rever'd abroad:[4]

If Scotland—and America—would return to such scenes, we are sure to enjoy God's rich blessings once more. Let us love the Word of God, for true faith is built on the testimony of the Apostles of Jesus.

## True Faith Produces Union with Christ

> "The glory that you have given me I have given to them, that they may be one even as we are one, I in them and you in me, that they may become perfectly one, so that the world may know that you sent me and loved them even as you loved me" (John 17:22-23).

The Father is in Jesus. Jesus is in the Father. And Jesus' disciples are in God. What a powerful verse! This speaks of the doctrine of union with Christ.

In the teaching of Paul, the believer is united with Christ in His life, in His sufferings, in His death, in His resurrection and in His future.

> Indeed, I count everything as loss because of the surpassing worth of knowing Christ Jesus my Lord. For his sake I have suffered the loss of all things and count them as rubbish, in order that I may gain Christ and be found in him, not having a righteousness of my own that comes from the law, but that which comes through faith in Christ, the righteousness from God that depends on faith— that I may know him and the power of his resurrection, and may share his sufferings, becoming like him in his death, that by any means possible I may attain the resurrection from the dead. Not that I have already obtained this or am already perfect, but I press on to make it my own, because Christ Jesus has made me his own. Brothers, I do not consider that I have made it my own. But one thing I do: forgetting what lies behind and straining forward to what lies ahead, I press on toward the goal for the prize of the upward call of God in Christ Jesus (Philippians 3:8-14).

The Father in Me and I am in the Father and they are in Us—this is union language.

[4] Lines 163 and 164 of "The Cotter's Saturday Night," from Robert Burns, *Poems, Chiefly in the Scottish Dialect* (Kilmarnock, 1786). http://eir.library.utoronto.ca/rpo/display/poem323.html .

I can't illustrate this better than with the example of married couples. According to Ephesians 5, when we are married, our lives are united. My life is bound up with Mae's life and vice versa. In fact, Paul says,

> "Therefore a man shall leave his father and mother and hold fast to his wife, and the two shall become one flesh." This mystery is profound, and I am saying that it refers to Christ and the church (Ephesians 5:31-32).

This is a fact. True faith unites you with Jesus Christ. What are the implications of that? It is the truth of John 10. You are in the palm of His hand; He will never let you go.

This brings true assurance. Charles Haddon Spurgeon preached this truth greatly when he said,

> "You are one with Him. You were 'buried in Him in baptism unto death,' wherein also you have risen with Him. You were crucified with Him upon the cross, you have gone up into heaven with Him, for He has raised us up together, and made us to sit together in the heavenly places in Christ Jesus. And surely you shall be actually in your very person with Him where He is, that you may behold His glory. You are one with Him."[5]

Here is the powerful effect of our union with Christ. If you are a member of His body, then you cannot be severed from Him. "Who shall separate you from the love of Christ?"[6] And the answer is, No one. If you can become undone from Christ, then just as you would press the rerun button on your VCR, you would have to rerun the old story of redemption. Jesus would have be removed from His throne, go back down to earth, back into the grave, back to the cross, and the nails would have to return to his hands. He would have to take back His words, "It is finished." And my beloved, that is not going to happen. If you are His, then you are His forever. You cannot be lost. And that is a fact.

[5] *Sermons of C. H. Spurgeon*, vol. x, p. 22 as quoted in the article, "Believer's Vital Union with Christ," http://www.abideinchrist.com/selah/nov29.html.

[6] Romans 8:35

## True Faith Bears Witness to the World

Jesus prayed for us, that we would be one with Him and each other, so that the world might believe. The faith for which Jesus prays is to be deposited in the disciples, but it is to have a radiating effect in the world

This is an interesting passage. Throughout the prayer, the world is seen as the antagonistic or uninterested and unregenerate people of this present evil age who oppose Jesus. But now here is a prayer that they may know. This accords with Jesus' earlier command to His disciples that the way the world will know is that we love one another.

And what does Jesus want the world to know?

### That God the Father sent Jesus Christ

The knowledge of Jesus must be spread throughout all of the earth. Whenever the gospel goes forth, it saves—but it also condemns. The church is like Isaiah who was given a unique mission,

> ..."Go, and say to this people: "'Keep on hearing, but do not understand; keep on seeing, but do not perceive.' Make the heart of this people dull, and their ears heavy, and blind their eyes; lest they see with their eyes, and hear with their ears, and understand with their hearts, and turn and be healed" (Isaiah 6:9-10).

Likewise, we preach; and if the gospel doesn't save, it prepares for judgment. This is not our work but the work of the Lord.

Jesus said, speaking of Himself,

> "And when he comes, he will convict the world concerning sin and righteousness and judgment" (John 16:8).

All over the world today there are little churches and great churches preaching Christ. The Spirit is scattering the saints of God to the ends of the earth that they may know about Jesus. Some will be saved from the judgment of God coming upon this earth, and some will be sealed for judgment. How will you respond? May your heart be opened by God to see your condition and turn to the living God, cry out in repentance, and rest in the Savior Jesus Christ. He came to save sinners.

### That the world may know the love of God the Father

> "I in them and you in me, that they may become perfectly one, so that the world may know that you sent me and loved them even as you loved me" (John 17:23).

God wants the world to know about a love that is completely different from any other love, about a love that can be grasped, experienced, and understood by people in the world. Jesus is calling people out of this world into His kingdom, and this kind of love will do it.

Years ago in Kansas, I saw this love, I saw this power, I saw this force at work in the life of my pastor. The closer I got to him, the more I saw this love at work.

I saw this love lived out with his wife, with his children, and when things turned against him, God turned those very things so that he ended up being blessed by the things that hurt him. He saw that God was so in control that whatever came against him, God would use it for His glory. He was not his own. He had been purchased with a price. He was his Lord's. That drew me and I wanted that God in my life. I wanted that power at work in my life. Jesus' prayer for me to know Him was being answered by the life of my pastor.

Is your life an answer to this prayer?

## True Faith Is a Love Like No Other

We are told that the Father loves His disciples like He loves Jesus.

> "I in them and you in me, that they may become perfectly one, so that the world may know that you sent me and loved them even as you loved me" (John 17:23).

The other day a college student asked what this meant. I am not sure I can fully answer it. And I think that when we have answered it, we are merely at the foothills of glory. Because this is a majestic and awesome saying that God the Father loves you the way He loves His only Son.

This is a love like no other. This is a love like no love on earth. It is a love between Father and Son that is demonstrated in human lives. We are gifts. Therefore, the objects of His affection are objects of His affection because of the love God the Father has for God the Son.

One of our elders told me that when he was a little boy, he had to take a bath in a #10 washtub. One day he put the water into the tub, got in, and realized that he had no soap. He then saw a bar of soap that his sister's boyfriend had carved into bird as a gift to her. He should have never taken that carved soap bird! His sister lit in on him and just about killed him before his brother pulled her off! Why did she get so bent out of shape over a piece of soap? You know the answer. That soap was the objection of her affection because it was a gift from the one she loved. And this is what Jesus is praying about.

When you are in Christ, you have shown yourself to be that gift of God. And He loves you because you remind Him of His Son.

The whole of the Word of God shows how God loves His people. But the Bible is also consistent in showing that God's people are mostly very unlovable, with few exceptions. Abraham was a coward who used his wife to cover his own hide. He was given a covenant that would bring forth a land and a nation in order to bring forth a Messiah to a world in need. However, Abraham introduced tremendous pain and heartache into his life by not trusting God for Isaac. But Abraham was the gift of the Father to the Son. David was the shepherd boy who became king. But David disobeyed God. He disobeyed God by taking more wives than one. He disobeyed God by taking another man's wife. His disobedience brought him great pain. But David was the apple of God's eye because David was a treasured gift from Father to Son. Peter was a braggadocios, boastful, bombastic blasphemer who was wrong on many counts. In Galatians Paul said that he withstood Peter face-to-face because he was wrong! Even as an apostle, Peter denied grace. But Jesus would never give up on Peter. Why? Because Peter was a gift from Father to Son. Listen to God way back in Deuteronomy:

> The LORD did not set his affection on you and choose you because you were more numerous than other peoples, for you were the fewest of all peoples. But it was because the LORD loved you and kept the

> oath he swore to your forefathers that he brought you out with a mighty hand and redeemed you from the land of slavery, from the power of Pharaoh king of Egypt (Deuteronomy 7:7-8, NIV).

Listen to how the Lord loves sinners in Zephaniah:

> Sing, O Daughter of Zion; shout aloud, O Israel! Be glad and rejoice with all your heart, O Daughter of Jerusalem! The LORD has taken away your punishment, he has turned back your enemy. The LORD, the King of Israel, is with you; never again will you fear any harm (Zephaniah 3:14-15, NIV).
>
> "The LORD your God is with you, he is mighty to save. He will take great delight in you, he will quiet you with his love, he will rejoice over you with singing" (Zephaniah 3:17, NIV).

And you wonder how God could love you, could rejoice over you and sing? If you knew me the way I know me, you would say, "How can God love this guy Milton? What is there to rejoice and sing over?" Here is the answer. It is not because you are the greatest, or the best, or the smartest, or the most gifted. The answer is that God chose you in love to be a gift from Father to Son. And gifts of love are precious to the one who gives and the one who receives.

## CONCLUSION

How do you know that Jesus is praying for you? How do you know that you are the object of God's affection?

She described herself as a "left-wing hippie type." She had been living on a small boat at a marina in Marin Country, California. She was an alcoholic recovering from the pain of an abortion. She was raised to be an atheist by an atheist. Her grandparents had been Presbyterian missionaries to Japan, but her father thought Christians, and especially Bible-believing Presbyterians, were right there with snake oil salesmen. She was the least likely to ever be a Christian. But on Sunday mornings, in the streets of her city, in the depth of her pain, she could hear the music of St. Andrews Presbyterian Church, a mostly black, inner city congregation in Marin City. She was drawn to the doorway and would go there to listen. She listened for about a year or so. The minister talked a lot about Jesus. It took over a year for her to come to that point, but she knew Jesus was calling her to come to Him for salvation. She wanted what her father had denied her: faith and baptism. But, thinking of how she wasn't free from alcohol and drugs, she told the pastor, "I am not good enough yet." The pastor responded, "You're putting the cart before the horse. So-honey? Come on down."

She did. But she didn't walk an aisle. Jesus walked the aisle and came to her when she couldn't make a move to Him.

> "I became aware of someone with me, hunkered down in the corner." She knew it was Jesus. "I felt him just sitting there on his haunches in the corner of my sleeping loft, watching me with patience and love.' For the next few days she sensed Jesus following her everywhere, [as she put it]'like a little cat.' Finally, she writes, 'I took a long deep breath and said out loud, 'All right. You can come in.'"[7]

Anne Lamott became what Jesus prayed for her: one of His own. She wrote *Traveling Mercies: Some Thoughts on Faith*.[8] This book of essays describing how God's love in choosing sinners can give anyone hope became a best seller. She teaches Sunday school and Communicant's Class. Her twelve-year-old son is being reared to know Christ. She says of her life in the local church,

> "I'm kind of like an awkward-shaped tile for the bathroom," she says, describing her role in the church. "Wherever they need a tile, I can fill in."[9]

She still strikes me as being a bit left of center, but I bet she would think that I was a little weird, too. And she would be right. But her story, in the midst of so much confusion about what is faith, is a beautiful example of what God is doing. Annie Lamott wrote of her faith,

> "How did some fabulously cerebral and black-humored cynic like myself come to fall for all that Christian lunacy, to see the cross not as an end but a beginning, to believe as much as I believe in gravity or in the size of space that Jesus paid a debt he didn't owe because we had a debt we couldn't

---

[7] Eva Stimson, *Anne Lamott's Subversive Faith* [Internet] (Presbyterians Today, June 2002 [cited March 3 2005]); http://www.pcusa.org/today/cover/june02/cover.htm.

[8] Anne Lamott, *Traveling Mercies: Some Thoughts on Faith*, 1st ed. (New York: Pantheon Books, 1999).

[9] Stimson, *Anne Lamott's Subversive Faith*.

> pay? It, my faith, is a great mystery. It has all the people close to me shaking their heads. It has *me* shaking my head."[10]

Today, you don't need to walk an aisle. Jesus will do all the walking. But will you open your heart to a faith that defies everything, that says, "this can't be true." You see, Jesus is praying for you. He is praying, not that you will find faith, but that faith will find you. And dazzle you. And defy your imaginations. And welcome you into the company of other sinners who don't deserve this love.

Don't put the cart before the horse. "Come on down"—just the way you are. He will accept you and love you. The cross is the beginning, not the end. There is nothing else in the world like this love.

[10] *The Meaning of Faith* [Internet] (American Public Media, 2004 [cited March 3 2005]); available from http://speakingoffaith.publicradio.org/programs/2003/04/11_faith/.

# Questions for Reflection

1. Can we defend from Scripture the first point that true faith begins with the prayer of Jesus?" Discuss it or think about it as you read this John 17 prayer once more.

2. Think back to how you were brought into the kingdom of God. Maybe it was as a covenant child. Or as a young person. Or as an adult. How did testimony play a part in your conversion? Whose testimony was used by God to reach you for Christ and what were the circumstances surrounding the testimony?

3. Think again about the doctrine of our union in Christ. How is this doctrine expressed in John 17? What are the practical benefits of this doctrine in your life today?

4. What impedes the Church from being an instrument of testimony that the world may know of Jesus Christ? How do we remedy this and become conveyers of His grace to others?

## Prayer

Lord of love, whose love is displayed in this beautiful prayer between Father and Son, open my hear today to receive Your love. Open my mind to contemplate, in quiet prayer, the power of love to transform the darker areas of my life. Open my life to see how I could be used to be Your testimony in the world today. For the sake of the gospel and in the name of the Lord.

*Amen.*

"He was so wholly given up to Your service, that He refused not the worst and hardest part of it, even bleeding, groaning, dying work; His love to you sweetened all this to Him."

**John Flavel**

"He set himself apart for you believers, and no others; no, not for angels, but for you: Will ye also set yourselves apart peculiarly for Christ? Be His, and no others? Let not Christ and the world share and divide your hearts in two halves betwixt them: let not the world step in and say, half mine. You will never do Christ right, nor answer this grace, till you can say, as it is, Psal. lxxiii. 25. 'Whom have I in heaven but Thee? And on earth there is none that I desire in comparison of Thee.' None but Christ, none but Christ, is a proper motto for a Christian."

**John Flavel**

# 5

# HUMBLED TO DEATH

## John 17:1-5, 11, 24-26

Humility is a word we will not find in the High Priestly Prayer of Jesus in John 17. We will just find it demonstrated, lived out in this prayer. What we will see today will bring us closer to understanding the call to humility and what that call will bring about in our lives.

> When Jesus had spoken these words, he lifted up his eyes to heaven, and said, "Father, the hour has come; glorify your Son that the Son may glorify you, since you have given him authority over all flesh, to give eternal life to all whom you have given him. And this is eternal life, that they know you the only true God, and Jesus Christ whom you have sent. I glorified you on earth, having accomplished the work that you gave me to do. And now, Father, glorify me in your own presence with the glory that I had with you before the world existed" (John 17:1-5).
>
> "And I am no longer in the world, but they are in the world, and I am coming to you. Holy Father, keep them in your name, which you have given me, that they may be one, even as we are one" (John 17:11).
>
> "Father, I desire that they also, whom you have given me, may be with me where I am, to see my glory that you have given me because you loved me before the foundation of the world. O righteous Father, even though the world does not know you, I know you, and these know that you have sent me. I made known to them your name, and I will continue to make it known, that the love with which you have loved me may be in them, and I in them" (John 17:24-26).

## THE IMAGE OF HUMILITY

Recently I was at a fundraiser where autographed pictures of sports heroes were being auctioned. I looked at them and could imagine a signed photo of the great golfer Phil Michelson hanging on my wall. Seeing Phil each day would motivate me to hang in there through all eighteen holes every day. But it was too expensive. Then I saw an autographed action photo of Vince Lombardi, the great Green Bay Packers football coach. Boy, that would have looked great, inspiring me to inspire others in my pastorate. But the price for Vince was also out of my reach. I really liked the shot of Peyton Manning throwing the ball and I just knew that seeing Peyton Manning every day would help me to realize what we all want—to be an all-pro pastor. But when the bidding was done, Phil Michelson, Vince Lombardi, and the Peyton Manning were hanging on someone else's wall.

But what hangs on the walls of the greats? What picture would Albert Einstein have hung on his wall? I read that for most of his career Albert Einstein kept the portraits of two scientists on the wall—Newton and Maxwell. However, toward the end of his life he replaced those portraits with Gandhi and Albert Schweitzer. He said that it is time to replace the image of success with the image of service.

Isn't it time we replace the image of success in the Christian life with the image of service?

A.W. Tozer surveyed the condition of evangelical Christianity in North America in the mid-twentieth century, and he thought that a new cross was beginning to emerge.

> The old cross slew men; the new cross entertains them. The old cross condemned; the new cross amuses. The old cross destroyed confidence in the flesh; the new cross encourages it.[1]

The Word of God is replete with teaching about humility.

> The fear of the Lord is instruction in wisdom
> And humility comes before honor (Proverbs 15:33).

[1] http://www.sermonillustrations.com/a-z/c/cross.htm.

In Philippians 2, a passage we have referred to many times in our study on John 17, Paul taught,

> Do nothing from rivalry or conceit, but in humility count others more significant than yourselves (Philippians 2:3).

This is an absolute impossibility for a self-centered person like myself, unless the Holy Spirit does something in my life.

When I counsel people about things that are going on in their lives, I always try to isolate a particular portion of God's Word and lift out the changeless, timeless truth of that Word to apply to their unique situation. This past week I was counseling with a family. The problem they were facing caused me to look to 1 Peter 5:5-6.

> Likewise, you who are younger, be subject to the elders. Clothe yourselves, all of you, with humility toward one another, for "God opposes the proud but gives grace to the humble." Humble yourselves, therefore, under the mighty hand of God so that at the proper time he may exalt you, (1 Peter 5:5-6).

When humility comes into play in the Christian life, the opposing forces are defanged. They are robbed of their power by the humility of the believer who says, Lord, I can't fight this fight; You are going to have to deal with this. And thus the next verse in Peter:

> casting all your anxieties on him, because he cares for you (1 Peter 5:7).

Humility leads to success in the Christian life, but that success cannot be measured by what we see in the world. Nowhere do we see this more than in John 17. Here is the picture of humility. Here is the King of kings and the Lord of lords, the One to whom every knee shall bow and every tongue confess that He is Lord, the One who relinquished the glory of heaven (though He never relinquished His divinity) in order to come on behalf of sinful man and face the cross where He will die for the sinner, Jesus Christ, at prayer with His heavenly Father. The greatness of the Lord Jesus Christ is tied to his humiliation. Philippians 2 is teaching this.

> Have this mind among yourselves, which is yours in Christ Jesus, who, though he was in the form of God, did not count equality with God a

> thing to be grasped, but made himself nothing, taking the form of a servant, being born in the likeness of men. And being found in human form, he humbled himself by becoming obedient to the point of death, even death on a cross (Philippians 2:5-8).

Here Paul describes His humiliation. But in the second part of the passage he says,

> Therefore God has highly exalted him and bestowed on him the name that is above every name, so that at the name of Jesus every knee should bow, in heaven and on earth and under the earth, and every tongue confess that Jesus Christ is Lord, to the glory of God the Father (Philippians 2:9-11).

In the world of self-actualizing, success-driven athletes and business people, we must return to the cross. No true greatness, nothing of eternal value can come out of the strength of man. We must rely on the strength of God, and this calls for humility. No one was greater than Jesus Christ; yet, Jesus modeled greatness through humility.

In John 17 there are three ways greatness is modeled through humility.

## Jesus Models Humility in His Role as the Son

God the Son is equal with God the Father in every part of His being. Yet, He shows humility in accepting this role relationship within the Godhead. He does only what His Father calls Him to do, and He says that He has accomplished what the Father has given Him to do. All of His words in John 17 about accomplishing what the Father has given Him to do come to fruition with Jesus' words on the cross: "It is finished,"[2]

In Philippians 2, Paul tells us that we are to esteem others as higher than ourselves. This brings unity, and it brings a building up of the church that in turn can reach out to the world, and the world will actually be able to receive the Word of God because it comes in humility. Paul says that we are to have the same mind as Jesus, so following Jesus in His prayer of humility in His role as the Son has a practical value for us today.

How are we living out our roles in life? Is there envy over our bosses? Bitterness over the authority that God has given to our parents, to the

[2] John 19:30

government, or to our spouses? The way to greatness in the Christian life is through humility in our relationships. The very mission of the church and the purpose of our lives are related to the way we are living out humility in relationships.

Most important is humility in our relationship to God. God is our Father. We are not autonomous creatures. We were created by God for God, and we are never complete until we come to Him as children in need of Him. So reaching our destiny means living in a right relationship with our heavenly Father through believing in His Son and following Him.

But we need to see that God calls us to right relationships with others as well. There will never be a truly successful man or woman, a truly great person, unless that person gives his life away for others. Children and youth, God is calling you to greatness through humility in your relationship with your parents, your teachers, and the other authorities in your lives. The devil tells you that greatness is in being independent of authority, unruly, being about your own business. But Jesus shows us that greatness begins with humility in relationship to authority. For even the Son of God delighted in only doing what His father commanded.

> The young seminarian was excited about preaching his first sermon in his home church. After three years in seminary, he felt adequately prepared, and when he was introduced to the congregation, he walked boldly to the pulpit, his head high, radiating self-confidence.
>
> But he stumbled reading the Scriptures and then lost his train of thought halfway through the message. He began to panic, so he did the safest thing: He quickly ended the message, prayed, and walked dejectedly from the pulpit, his head down, his self-assurance gone.
>
> Later, one of the godly elders whispered to the embarrassed young man, "If you had gone up to the pulpit the way you came down, you might have come down the way you went up." The elder was right. God still resists the proud but gives grace to the humble.[3]

[3] http://www.bible.org/illus.asp?topic_id=756.

Every believer, knowing that we are saved by grace, kept by God's power, and totally dependent upon His sovereign power, must be the most broken, most humble of creatures. And this is the posture of the man or the woman who will be used by God.

Like Jesus, we are called to be humble sons and daughters. Only those will be used greatly. The power of Christ comes through broken vessels.

## Jesus Modeled Humility in His Role as Servant

Jesus is about to go through humiliation on the cross in order to obtain glory in the resurrection. Glory is an important and frequently used word in John 17. Just studying the word glory in this passage will lead us to understand the servanthood of the Lord Jesus.

> When Jesus had spoken these words, he lifted up his eyes to heaven, and said, "Father, the hour has come; glorify your Son that the Son may glorify you," (John 17:1).
>
> "I glorified you on earth, having accomplished the work that you gave me to do" (John 17:4).
>
> "And now, Father, glorify me in your own presence with the glory that I had with you before the world existed" (John 17:5).
>
> "All mine are yours, and yours are mine, and I am glorified in them" (John 17:10).
>
> "The glory that you have given me I have given to them, that they may be one even as we are one," (John 17:22).
>
> "Father, I desire that they also, whom you have given me, may be with me where I am, to see my glory that you have given me because you loved me before the foundation of the world" (John 17:24).

Admittedly, the way Jesus uses the word glory is a little confusing. He talks about a glory He had with the Father before the foundation of the world, a glory which has been relinquished and which He will assume once again at His ascension. He talks about yet a different kind of glory that He has shared with others, and in fact, that he has deposited into His disciples, the glory that somehow His disciples may share.

Glory is best understood by looking first to the Old Testament.

When Moses cried out to see God's glory, God passed in front of him. Clearly, God's glory is the very person and presence of the Almighty. When King Solomon was dedicating the Temple of the Lord, the glory of the Lord filled the place. Here the glory of God is not just His person, but also His presence. And in the wake of His presence, there is awe and wonder in the senses of those who experience Him.

Now, here is the amazing thing. Jesus has to ask that God glorify Him. There was a time when He basked in that glory of God. But something happened. God the Son never stopped being God, but He put off His royal robes of glory in order to become man. This is humility that leads to exaltation. Love drove Him to shed glory and then to ask for it again. Where would His glory be given to Him? On the cross. Paul says that is the mind that should be in His disciples. This accords with what Jesus told His disciples. He pointed to the ostentatious behavior and conceited demands of the religious leaders of that day and said that it must not be so with His people. Rather, Jesus said,

> "The greatest among you shall be your servant. Whoever exalts himself will be humbled, and whoever humbles himself will be exalted" (Matthew 23:11-12).

Hudson Taylor was scheduled to speak at a large Presbyterian church in Melbourne, Australia. The moderator of the service introduced the missionary in eloquent and glowing terms. He told the large congregation all that Taylor had accomplished in China, and then presented him as "our illustrious guest." Taylor stood quietly for a moment, and then opened his message by saying, "Dear friends, I am the little servant of an illustrious Master."[4]

That is the testimony of a servant. I pray that is mine. For if Jesus lived to express God's glory, we must ever live to reflect His glory and His glory alone. We are little servants of an illustrious Master.

## Jesus Modeled Humility in His Role as the Sacrifice

It was the hour of suffering and death, even the death of the cross. He had accomplished all that the Father had given Him to do in terms of

[4] *Wycliffe Handbook of Preaching and Preachers*, W. Wiersbe, p. 243.

disclosing His Father's will to His disciples who would now make it known to the world. He had accomplished the Father's will in that He had lived the perfect life, He had satisfied righteousness. But now He anticipated the cross when he said, "I am no longer in the world," thus anticipating the crucifixion, anticipating the time when He would announce, "It is finished." The sacrifice for sins is complete. He has not only lived the life, He has died the death for our sins.

Our Savior who died also calls us to die to ourselves. We cannot be a sacrifice. We cannot redeem anything by giving away our lives. Yet, as Bonhoeffer said, "When Christ calls a man, He bids him come and die."

I was born and reared in the South, but I came to appreciate the people of the Midwest for the many years that I lived there. I heard and read many stories of courage, but one that fascinates me is the story of a prairie woman and her infant who were out in a vast field on the prairie. A great fire began to rage, as they sometimes do in the summer, from a lightening strike. She ran this way and that way but found herself surrounded by the fire. She took the baby off of her back and dug a hole in the earth. She placed the baby in the hole prostrated her body over it. As the fire raged, it came upon her, and she became a sacrifice in the fire so that the baby could live.[5]

The cross was the place of sacrifice where the wrath of God against sin raged against the Son of God so that you could live. We must never remove this from our faith. It is not only how our Lord saved us; sacrifice is the way that we must relate to each other and to the world.

## CONCLUSION

Jesus showed humility as a Son, as a servant, and as a sacrifice. Shall we not live in humility before God and men?

Humility is modeled and lived through sacrifice. Some of the most amazing examples of how humility produced greatness can be seen in the founders of our nation. Here were men and women, many of whom were at the top of their field, who sacrificed everything and

[5] Unknown source.

channeled every gift that came to them, every influence, every financial opportunity through the narrow opening of a burden and a vision.

Some time ago, I was asked by the Daughters of the American Revolution in Kansas to give a speech about the role of chaplains in the American Revolution. I took that call as a great honor and conducted no small amount of research on the topic. What I found was not only of interest but it also amazed me. I found one after another examples of clergymen who led the men in their congregations off to war, fought in the war, and then continued building and founding a nation.

John Gano, the husband of Sarah and father of eleven children, was pastor of First Baptist Church of New York City in 1762 and became Chaplain to the 19th Continental Infantry on January 1, 1776. He later became chaplain to men in his own congregation when he served the 5th New York Infantry, where he became Brigade Chaplain. At the occasion of the cessation of hostilities, he offered thanksgiving by order of General Washington. He returned to the pastorate, but also felt led to do more for his nation. So he founded Brown University.

Andrew Hunter, Jr., a Presbyterian, was a graduate of Princeton and was a pastor in New Jersey. He was a delegate to the first Presbyterian General Assembly in 1789. He became a trustee of Princeton and then, at the beginning of the war, became Chaplain to a battalion from New Jersey and served in several other units as well. He was taken prisoner but escaped and returned to battle as chaplain of another unit. He was present at the Battle of Yorktown and received personal thanks from General Washington for his valiant service at the Battle of Monmouth. He retired back to the pastorate and helped found the United States Naval Academy. But something kept driving him, and he entered service as Chaplain again in the War of 1812. He became Senior Naval Chaplain.

Samuel Kirkland, a Congregationalist minister, was also a Princeton graduate. He had a burden to reach Indians with the gospel. He learned Mohawk, Seneca, and Oneida languages. At the American Revolution he served as a Chaplain to the American forces. He went on to found Hamilton College.

You wonder, What does that have to do with John 17 or me? These men, and so many others like them, were educated at the finest institutions available, were called upon to serve great churches, became leaders in a war for independence, and then afterward laid the foundations of a new nation. They literally gave everything they had, they humbled themselves to death, to see a nation become a reality. They did so because they were convicted by a Savior who died for them.

And shall it be said of us, They used what they were given to...have some really nice vacations. Or, They were so moved by the love of Christ that they listened to more tapes and read more books. Or, shall it be said, The love of Christ caused them to humble themselves in their generation to reach a lost world for Jesus Christ. They acted as if they were controlled by another power, a power that is not of this world, but which brought blessing and beauty to this world. They literally humbled themselves to death—just like their illustrious Master.

Humility is not weakness. Humility is taking all of the strength and putting it under the cover a burden and a vision. It is channeling all of the resources available to you for a cause that is greater than yourself, for a vision that is greater than yourself. May God bless us with humility that will bring greatness in His kingdom. But that will begin with you prostrate before Jesus Christ in your heart.

# Questions for Reflection

1. Go through the passage again. Mark the places where you find humility exhibited by Jesus. Think through each of them or talk about them in this way: How can this kind of humility be evident in our lives? What does this humility signify? Why is it important?

2. Is it possible for our relationship with God, as His children, to lead to pride? How?

3. What does glory mean in this passage, for example in John 17:22? How is it that the glory Jesus was given could be given to us?

4. How does the servanthood and sacrifice of Jesus transfer to our lives? What are the limits of these attributes? What are the ways in which we can follow Him in these areas? What is the power to put on these roles?

## Prayer

Savior and Lord, whose glory is shown in exaltation as well as humiliation, I bow before You this day as I seek to understand Your great sacrifice for sinners like me. I bow before You and plead that, by Your grace; I might know something of the life of love I see in You. Grant that the ugly parts of my life would be overwhelmed by the beauty of Jesus and finally be removed. In the name of Jesus.

*Amen.*

"Ruthless trust ultimately comes down to this: faith in the person of Jesus and hope in His promise. In spite of all disconcerting appearances, we stare down death without nervousness and anticipate resurrection solely because Jesus has said, 'You have My word on it.' It doesn't get any more ruthless. Either we believe in the resurrection and therefore trust in Jesus of Nazareth and the Gospel He preached, or we do not believe in the resurrection and therefore do not trust in Jesus of Nazareth and the Gospel He preached."

**Brennan Manning**

"Trust in God and trust in Me."

**John 14.1**

# 6

# TRUSTING IN THE CHRIST WHO PRAYS FOR YOU

### Psalm 18:28; Isaiah 42:16; John 17:20-26

A winner of an academy award looked down at a little old lady in the audience, thanked her and said, "My mamma believed in me when no one else believed in me."

When you stand before Almighty God and you hear, "Acquitted," and you are ushered into the heavenly Jerusalem, you will say, "There was One who believed in me, who prayed for me. I wouldn't be here without that One." In John 17, we learn that One is Jesus.

Hear the testimony of David.

> For it is you who light my lamp; the Lord my God lightens my darkness (Psalms 18:28).

God's Messiah, who is prophesied here in Isaiah, tells us His mission.

> And I will lead the blind in a way that they do not know, in paths that they have not known I will guide them. I will turn the darkness before them into light, the rough places into level ground. These are the things I do, and I do not forsake them (Isaiah 42:16).

In the Old Testament the testimony of David, who went through trying and troubling times, says that the only light on his path is the Lord. In Isaiah we see that the very mission of the Messiah was to give light and sight to those who were blind and hearing to those who are spiritually dead. Then in John 17 we read the prayer of our Lord Jesus as He prays for you.

> "I do not ask for these only, but also for those who will believe in me through their word, that they may all be one, just as you, Father, are in me, and I in you, that they also may be in us, so that the world may believe that you have sent me. The glory that you have given me I have given to them, that they may be one even as we are one, I in them and you in me, that they may become perfectly one, so that the world may know that you sent me and loved them even as you loved me. Father, I desire that they also, whom you have given me, may be with me where I am, to see my glory that you have given me because you loved me before the foundation of the world. O righteous Father, even though the world does not know you, I know you, and these know that you have sent me. I made known to them your name, and I will continue to make it known, that the love with which you have loved me may be in them, and I in them" (John 17:20-26).

## MOVING BEYOND UNDERSTANDING

The brilliant ethicist, John Kavanagh, went to work for three months in the "house of the dying" in Calcutta seeking for answers on how to spend the rest of his life. Mother Theresa was still alive then, carrying the crippled, pouring oil onto the wounds that would never heal and giving dignity to a people who are called outcasts. John Kavanaugh, on his first day there, went to Mother Theresa. "And what can I do for you?" She asked. Kavanaugh asked for prayer. Mother Theresa asked, "What do you want me to pray for?" The scholar replied, "Pray that I have clarity." She said firmly, "No, I will not do that." In surprise to this abrupt answer by this tiny Albanian nun, John Kavanaugh said, "Why not?" And Mother Theresa told him, "Clarity is the last thing you are clinging to and must let go of." The man said that she seemed to have clarity and understanding in abundance. And he wanted it, too. She laughed and said, "I have never had clarity; what I have always had is trust. So I will pray that you trust God."[1]

---

[1] Brennan Manning, *Ruthless Trust: The Ragamuffin's Path to God* (San Francisco: HarperSanFrancisco, 2002) 5.

There comes a time in our lives when we don't need more Bible understanding. We need trust. For several weeks we have been studying the unfathomable love of God, the deep, deep love of Jesus in John 17. We cannot plumb the depths of this magnificent passage. When we have done our best, we have only come to the foothills of glory in this passage. We really don't understand it fully, but there comes a time when our understanding must yield to faith, to trust. Now is that time.

Jesus' prayer is that you will trust in Him. He prays for those who will believe. But I want to replace the word believe with the word trust. In an area with such a rich biblical heritage, it is easy to say, Everybody believes in Jesus. But do we understand the word believe? Do we understand the power of what that means in the New Testament. It is to recognize the authority of Jesus Christ and to surrender yourself totally to that authority.

Yet it is impossible for us, in and of ourselves, to trust in Jesus Christ. You can trust in Jesus because Jesus has prayed for you to trust in Him.

He did this in three remarkable ways in this passage.

## Jesus Prayed for You before You Were Born.

Jesus says,

> "I do not ask for these only, but also for those who will believe in me through their word," (John 17:20).

In other words, Jesus was praying for people who had not yet been born!

God also said to young Jeremiah,

> "Before I formed you in the womb I knew you, and before you were born I consecrated you; I appointed you a prophet to the nations" (Jeremiah 1:5).

This, likewise, accords with Paul in his letter to Ephesians:

> For he chose us in him before the creation of the world to be holy and blameless in his sight. In love he predestined us to be adopted as his sons through Jesus Christ, in accordance with his pleasure and will—(Ephesians 1:4-5, NIV).

Our Savior is praying for His little ones before they are yet born. We come to faith because Jesus prayed for faith in us even before we were born. It may seem remarkable that Christ knew you by name and prayed for you before you were born, but think of how we pray for each other and how we pray for the birth of children. We have several couples who are expecting a child right now, and I am joining them in prayer. I am praying for couples who are expecting a child that the wife is carrying. I am praying for two families who are expecting their child through the wonder of adoption. Let us consider, for a moment, the couples waiting on God's choice for them through adoption. They are praying for the child that God has chosen for them before the foundation of the earth. They are praying for safety in birth and for the day when that baby will be placed in their arms, and what a glorious time that is going to be in their lives. We are praying for someone not even born. In like manner, Jesus prayed for you to be adopted into His family before you were born.

After this prayer, after looking over a city that would reject Him, after riding into a city on the back of a donkey, hearing cries of "Hosanna!" which would become cries of "Crucify Him!" Jesus counted it all worth it. He counted it all worth it because He was praying for you.

You can trust our Lord, no matter your pain, no matter the pain you see in the world, because He first loved you. He loved you; He was speaking your name before you were born.

## Jesus Prayed for You before He Died for You.

Jesus prayed for your before He went to the cross. This is of enormous importance. It is important that you know that you were chosen in Christ before the foundation of the world and that your Savior called out your name to His Father in His life. He prayed for you, trusted in possessing you one day; therefore, He died for you. He did not die and then beg you to believe. He chose you, He prayed for you, and then He died for you. Your salvation is not dependent upon your choice of God but upon His choice of you.

> "You did not choose me, but I chose you and appointed you that you should go and bear fruit and that your fruit should abide, so that whatever you ask the Father in my name, he may give it to you" (John 15:16).
>
> "...no one can come to me unless the Father has enabled him" (John 6:65, NIV).

These are amazing words with mysterious meaning. But rather than theorizing about the mystery, let's see the practical power of this truth. These words are for your assurance that you who are standing afar may know that God has already taken the first step to you. That Jesus prayed for you before He ever died for you means the end of despair for you who are struggling to find faith, for you who are longing to trust. For you who have been abandoned by family, hurt by friends, brutalized by the rat race, or deeply moved by a world of suffering and pain, this Jesus is already on your side. He does not require that you get your questions answered before He comes to you. He comes to you in the midst of the pain and loves you. Jesus loved you and prayed for you and valued you above His own prerogatives for divinity, above His own sinless life. He was willing to be handed over to evil men, to be ridiculed, to be abandoned by God on the stinking and smoldering landfill called Calvary so that He might save those whom He loves.

To know this and experience this prayer of Jesus for you, will not only set free those who are longing to trust Jesus, but will bring happiness to sad hearts of disciples who have forgotten the wonder of His love.

Brenning Manning, in his book *Ruthless Trust,* tells of a time when he was speaking at Stanford University in Palo Alto, California. He had addressed faculty and students about the grace of God in Christ, focusing on the love of Jesus. The next day a distinguished faculty member came to him.

> "At one point in my life," she said, "I had a faith so strong that it shaped the very fiber of each day. I was conscious of God's presence even in stressful situations. The fire of Christ burned inside me. Slowly, though, and almost imperceptibly...."[2]

[2] Ibid., 18.

She told how that fire had gone out. She told how academia and life and stuff just crowded out trusting in Jesus.

> After a moment she continued: "After you spoke on the love of God last night, I cried for an hour. My life is so empty…I'm like Mary Magdalene in the garden crying, 'Where has my Beloved gone?' I miss God so much that sometimes I feel frantic. I long for the relationship I used to have?"[3]

Do you feel like Mary Magdalene— "Where has my Beloved gone?" Did you once follow Him closely, every day filled with trusting Him, but now other things have crowded in? The truth is, He is alive. He died and rose again, while you were still a sinner. And before He died for you, He even prayed for you. You can then trust Him for the first time or trust Him again. Your Beloved is here.

## Jesus Prayed for You Though Some of You Will Not Pray to Him.

He not only prayed for you before you were born, before He died for you, Jesus Christ prayed for you while you were still a sinner. The power of Christ's prayer is the power that causes you to believe.

Your unbelief or your lack of trust does not intimidate God, nor will the Father deny Jesus' prayer for you to trust in Him because you are now in sin or you are confused or you have troubles of the soul. No, my beloved, God is like Michangelo who saw Davids and Moses in rocks when others only saw boulders.

This whole magnificent chapter is about the step that God has taken to you before you ever took a step at all. He chose you, He loved you, He prayed for you, He died for you, and He believed in you.

He trusted in His oath and covenant and blood. He trusted in the design of His heavenly Father who chose you in love. He knew His mission on earth and on the cross would be successful because the Spirit would regenerate your dead spiritual heart and cause you to pant after Him. Again, this trust is way beyond anything you could imagine. It is rooted in the divine love of God for Himself and, thus, for His creation. That is

[3] Ibid.

> "To be grateful for an unanswered prayer, to give thanks in a state of interior desolation, to trust in the love of God in the face of the marvels, cruel circumstances, obscenities, and commonplaces of life is to whisper a doxology in the darkness."[4]

I will tell you about a doxology in the darkness, a grabbing onto faith when everything in your life says impossible. An Episcopal minister, Tom Minifie, lives and ministers in Seattle, Washington. I read of an encounter he had one Sunday with a high profile couple in his church who were sitting with their Down's syndrome baby. He sensed that they were uncomfortable with the baby in worship and seemed to just try to get to the door as quickly as possible. He saw them at the door and asked if they would wait for him to finish greeting the people and then meet with him in his office. They were confused and even uncomfortable, but they waited and met him in his office. There he asked if he could hold the baby. He took the child into his arms and began to sob. He looked into their eyes and asked them, "Do have any idea of the gift God has given you in this child?" The parents were confused and even hurt. But the pastor went on, as he held the baby close:

"Two years ago my three-year-old daughter, Sylvia, died with Down's syndrome. We have four other children, so we know the blessing that kids can be. Yet the most precious gift we've ever received in our entire lives was Sylvia. In her uninhibited expression of affection, she revealed to us the face of God as no other human being ever has. Treasure this child, for he will lead you into the heart of God." From that day forward, I read that the parents began to brag about their little one.[5]

Why do I tell you that story? Because I believe it illustrates how God brings us to trust Him. He does it, not by our expectations for the Messiah we think we want, but from the far reaches of doubt and despair that leads us to the Savior we need. We best believe, not from our positions of strength, but out of weakness. We even cradle our weaknesses—the broken dreams, the unexpected illness, the abandonment, the failure—because in our weakness we see the heart of God. In our weakness in sin, we see a Savior who prayed for us, died for us, and rose

[4] Ibid., 37.
[5] Ibid., 174-175.

again for us. It is in His life, His prayer for us, His trusting heart for us, that we come to know that we can trust Him or trust Him again.

Whatever you think is keeping you from Jesus is likely the thing that He is using to bring you to Him. This is possible because of the deep, deep love of Jesus.

We read in John 17 that He prayed for you. Will you now trust in Him that today His prayer is answered, once and for all, in your life?

# Questions for Reflection

1. What did Mother Theresa mean when she told John Kavanaugh, that she would not pray for clarity for him? Does knowing God's will for our lives always involve possessing a perfect clarity? What are some examples from your own life, or the life of a great Christian, where the beginning of a great journey of faith was marked by the actual absence of clarity?

2. Think back over your own life. How have the tough, bad, or even sinful things that have happened to you brought you closer to Christ?

3. Why do you believe that the clear and simple message of the love of God through the life and sacrificial death of Jesus Christ on the cross is so powerful?

4. Do you think that Christ prays for us today through the instrumentality of others? Who has prayed for you in your life? What has been the effect of those prayers?

5. Read back through the Conclusion of this chapter, about the little Downs Syndrome child. What do think is meant by the author's phrase, "to cradle our weakness?" How does that bring us closer to Christ? To each other? To the lost?

## Prayer

Lord, Your hands and feet are eternally pierced. Your side bears the marks of a spear. You come to me, fresh from the cross, reminding me of the price You paid for my sin. Teach me, through Your own heart shown so beautifully in this prayer, to receive You, again and again, in weakness and joy. Teach me that You use my weakness also to reach others. Cause me to open my hands and release my sorrows and pain to You, O Christ. Help me to offer all of my life as a living sacrifice to You. Lord, teach me to give my brokenness back to You, and use me to reach other broken people. In Jesus' name.

*Amen.*

## Michael A. Milton

In 2001, Dr. Michael A. Milton was called as the pastor of the historic First Presbyterian Church of Chattanooga, Tennessee, the twelfth in 161 years. As senior minister, he provides expository preaching, teaching, and worship leadership to a growing congregation in downtown Chattanooga. He also serves as staff leader to assistant pastors, directors, and volunteers in a multi-faceted ministry that includes a radio and television outreach, a vibrant departmental Sunday School ministry, an aggressive world missions program, a camping ministry, church planting, and an outreach to the nation through numerous local and national agencies and ministries. He can be heard on the *Faith for Living with Mike Milton* outreach ministry, which utilizes radio, television, iPod broadcasts, and Internet audio and video (faithforliving.net). Dr. Milton is the author of the books, *Leaving a Career to Follow a Call: A Vocational Guide to the Ordained Ministry, Authentic Christianity and the Life of Freedom* and *Discipleship in Babylon.* He has also written numerous popular and academic articles and published in such periodicals as *Preaching Magazine, The Journal of the Evangelical Theological Society, Annual Minister's Manual, The Christian Observer* and *World Magazine.* He has been featured on national radio and television programs such as *Truths that Transform* with Dr. D. James Kennedy, *The Coral Ridge Hour,* and Moody Radio's *Money Matters.* In 2005 Music for Missions released his first musical recording, *He Shall Restore.*

Prior to becoming Senior Pastor at First Presbyterian Church of Chattanooga, Dr. Milton served sixteen years in the business world and was also a top secret Navy linguist. He interned under D. James Kennedy at Coral Ridge Presbyterian Church and after seminary, planted two churches: Redeemer Presbyterian Church in Overland Park, Kansas; and Kirk O' the Isles Church in Savannah, Georgia. He also founded Westminster Academy Christian School in Overland Park and was the administrative head and a professor at Knox Theological Seminary. A graduate of Mid America Nazarene University (Kansas) and Knox Theological Seminary, in 1998 he earned a Doctor of Philosophy degree in theology and religious studies from The University of Wales (UK).

Dr. Milton's personal story of moving from orphan and prodigal son to understanding God's grace and receiving His adoption through Jesus Christ forms a frequent motif for offering Christ's healing to a broken generation. Often his sermons are illustrated with songs that he writes, sings, and performs with guitar.

In addition to his pastoral work, Dr. Milton holds a commission in the US Army Reserves as a chaplain, a ministry that he continues. Serving on several boards and active in a number of civic organizations, he also remains involved in preaching and teaching in churches, conferences, and seminaries. Dr. and Mrs. Milton and their son reside in the Chattanooga community.

# THE VISION AND MINISTRY OF FIRST PRESBYTERIAN CHURCH,

## Chattanooga, Tennessee

## and

# FAITH FOR LIVING

First Presbyterian Church of Chattanooga, Tennessee, has a burden for revival and reformation of our generation that God's glory may be known.

### The Core Values

- A passion for God's Word
- A heart for God's World
- A commitment to God's Grace
- And a desire to be an equipping church.

### The Vision

- To be a ministry of God's grace, with lives transformed through the gospel of Jesus Christ.

### The Mission

- which seeks to move to our vision, is to gather, grow and send forth strong disciples of Jesus Christ.

### The Philosophy of Ministry

- Expository Bible preaching
- Living worship
- Loving fellowship
- Compassionate outreach
- The priority of prayer.

## The Strategies

for seeking to fulfill this mission and realize this vision

- Maximize the Word of God so that every Bible message proclaimed and taught at our church is made available to as many people as possible through the means of print, radio and television and the Internet.

## Books in the

## Faith for Living: Sermons-in-Print Series

*Authentic Christianity and the Life of Freedom: Expository Messages from Galatians*

*The Demands of Discipleship: Expository Messages from Daniel*

## Other Books by

## Michael Milton

*Leaving a Career to Follow a Call: A Vocational Guide to the Ordained Ministry*